Springer Series in Information Sciences   16

Editor: Thomas S. Huang

Springer Series in Information Sciences

Editors: Thomas S. Huang   Manfred R. Schroeder

J. L. C. Sanz
E. B. Hinkle   A. K. Jain

Radon and Projection Transform-Based Computer Vision

Algorithms, A Pipeline Architecture, and Industrial Applications

With 39 Figures

Springer-Verlag Berlin Heidelberg New York
London Paris Tokyo

Dr. Jorge L. C. Sanz
Eric B. Hinkle

Computer Science Department, IBM Almaden Research Center
650 Harry Rd., San Jose, CA 95120-6099, USA

Professor Anil K. Jain

Electrical and Computer Engineering Department, University of California at Davis,
Davis, CA 95616, USA

Series Editors:

Professor Thomas S. Huang

Department of Electrical Engineering and Cordinated Science Laboratory,
University of Illinois, Urbana, IL 61801, USA

Professor Dr. Manfred R. Schroeder

Drittes Physikalisches Institut, Universität Göttingen, Bürgerstraße 42–44,
D-3400 Göttingen, Fed. Rep. of Germany

ISBN-13:978-3-642-73014-6   e-ISBN-13:978-3-642-73012-2
DOI: 10.1007/ 978-3-642-73012-2

2153/3150-543210

Preface

This book deals with novel machine vision architecture ideas that make real-time projection-based algorithms a reality. The design is founded on raster-mode processing, which is exploited in a powerful and flexible pipeline. We concern ourselves with several image analysis algorithms for computing: projections of gray-level images along linear patterns (i.e., the Radon transform) and other curved contours; convex hull approximations; the Hough transform for line and curve detection; diameters; moments and principal components, etc. Additionally, we deal with an extensive list of key image processing tasks, which involve generating: discrete approximations of the inverse Radon transform operator; computer tomography reconstructions; two-dimensional convolutions; rotations and translations; multi-color digital masks; the discrete Fourier transform in polar coordinates; autocorrelations, etc. Both the image analysis and image processing algorithms are supported by a similar architecture. We will also demonstrate the applicability of some of the above algorithms to the solution of various industrial visual inspection problems.

The algorithms and architectural ideas surveyed here unleash the power of the Radon and other non-linear transformations for machine vision applications. We provide fast methods to transform images into projection space representations and to backtrace projection-space information into the image domain. The novelty of this approach is that the above algorithms are suitable for implementation in a pipeline architecture. Specifically, random access memory and other dedicated hardware components which are necessary for implementation of classical techniques are not needed for our algorithms. The effectiveness of our approach and the feasibility of the proposed architecture are demonstrated by running some of the new algorithms in conventional short pipelines for image analysis and image processing.

The authors would like to thank Dr. Its'hak Dinstein (Beer-Sheva University), Dr. Dragutin Petkovic and other members of the Machine Vision Group (IBM Almaden Research Center), and Dr. K. Mohiuddin (IBM Research) for many useful discussions.

June, 1987   *The Authors*

Contents

1. Introduction

A frequently expressed view in image analysis is that a general purpose vision system must be capable of generating rich descriptions without knowledge of specific objects in a scene. Defining the capabilities of such systems has received considerable research attention in the past several years. It is recognized that issues of system engineering play an essential role in the successful development of large computer vision systems. Moreover, it has been observed that computational issues such as architectural limitations, file structures, etc., have to some extent impeded progress in other areas of computer vision [Redd78]. Pragmatic aspects of computer vision have been extensively discussed in connection to basic image analysis capabilities such as edge detection, shape representation, segmentation, etc. [Erma78, Etch83, Neva78]

Architectures for image analysis and computer vision continue to be an area of active and important research. Before we can prove or disprove a conjecture regarding a certain image analysis representation or control structure, we must have a system providing reasonably fast response [Redd78]. For example, important contributions to the theory of early processing in biological vision systems [Grim81, Hild83, Marr80] can now be analysed and tested computationally. This possibility is attributable to advances in large scale integration as applied to signal and image processing architectures. No less important is the impact of these system issues on applications of machine vision [Sanz]. Automated visual inspection, an important area of current research interest, constitutes a good example. The real-time processing constraints usually imposed by inspection tasks highlight the critical importance of architectures, efficient and flexible algorithms, data bases, sensing technology, and other system capabilitites of an inspection machine.

In the next section, we will briefly survey some machine vision architectures and other parallel computers. For an excellent review of current architectures and future prospects the reader is referred to [Uhr84]. Section 1.1 will be useful for the reader since it provides a reference point for the architecture work described in later chapters.

1.1 Machine Vision Architectures

Most machine vision applications involve high-speed processing for a wide variety of algorithms, which generally access large amounts of data and involve entirely different representations. In some problems, in order to meet the required performance, each individual step of the solving methodology must run at video-rate speeds. To achieve the desired performance, these algorithms must be supported by an underlying, special-purpose architecture. In this section, a survey of some machine vision architectures is presented. By "architectures for machine vision" we mean hardware structures for fast execution of image-oriented algorithms. In our discussion we will analyze some relevant characteristics of machine vision algorithms that strongly influence the selection and applicability of a particular architecture.

A common goal of machine vision systems is the derivation of symbolic information from pictorial data. This task goes beyond the transformations used in image processing problems. Image processing consists of image to image transformations for human analysis (e.g., enhancement, restoration), transmission and storage (e.g., data compression), or image formation from incomplete data (e.g., reconstruction) [Rose82, Rose84]. However, the extraction of symbolic information requires data structures other than the simple iconic representations encountered in image processing applications. These structures involve linked lists, circular lists, trees, and other general graphs. The multiplicity of data structures, the variety of operations which are performed on the data, and the real-time requirements make architectures and parallel computing some of the most challenging research topics in the field of machine vision.

Among the problems facing the designer of machine vision architectures is that of selecting and/or building the proper hardware which efficiently implements image-to-image, image-to-symbols, and purely symbolic operations [Foun86]. Due to the nature of these operations, the underlying architectural requirements are rather different. This makes it difficult to use a single architecture that succesfully implements all the above transformations. Consequently, we still do not have a formal mechanism for mapping algorithms onto optimal architectures. Some attempts have been made in [Foun86, Jami86, Yala85]. Many factors, like processor power, granularity, topology [Reev84], fault tolerance [Reev83a], cost, etc., have to be considered in evaluating the applicability of architectures to machine vision. In addition, relevant algorithmic properties (inherent parallelism, memory requirements, etc.) must be taken into account to formalize this matching. It is worth noting that, in the end, no unequivocal ranking can be achieved without experimental results [Foun86].

In addition to trying to map algorithms onto architectures, there is another approach which consists of designing application-specific architectures [Ruet86]. Due to the advances of VLSI technology and related design tools, this seems to be a more and more attractive methodology. On the other hand, VLSI technology also facilitates cost-effective fabrication of complex general-purpose processors and parallel fine-grained machines. Both VLSI trends are expected to yield new architectures in forthcoming years.

It is clear that any manipulation of images involves the processing of an extraordinary amount of data. Typical image sizes range from $512 \times 512 \times 8$ bits in industrial applications, to $4000 \times 4000 \times 8$ bits for several spectral bands in LANDSAT satellite images. These data have to be processed at high speeds. Obviously, most standard von-Neumann architectures are not capable of processing this amount of data at the required speeds. An important argument against the use of von-Neumann architectures relates to their inability to exploit the high regularity of image data and image operators. While this argument is true for low-level operations on iconic data, it is still a research topic for other representations such as trees and other graphs. Such considerations have led to active research and development in parallel image architectures. Great success has been obtained for image to image operations, for which a large number of architectures have been built.

In the remainder of this section, we will first classify machine vision architectures into certain categories. Some examples of existing machines will be given for each. We will also briefly discuss hardware building blocks for these systems, and comment on future research trends in the field.

Machine vision architectures can be classified according to different parameters, depending on whether the emphasis is on system control, processor communication, granularity of the architecture, or flow of data [Foun83, Dani81, Reev84]. In fact, the whole issue of computer architecture classification has received great attention from the community [Haen77]. A traditional classification proposed in [Flyn66] gives particular emphasis to control and flow of data, while other authors considered parameters such as word-length and the number of words which are processed in parallel [Feng72].

A common classification involving architecture control follows. We will not elaborate on particular examples, but just list them with appropriate references.

— Single instruction, single data stream (SISD). This group involves the standard "von-Neumann processor" where operations are performed sequentially on each data item. Examples include conventional microprocessors (8086, 68000 etc.) and also reduced instruction set computers (RISC). It is obvious that this architecture is not sufficient for low- and mid-level vision. It is most appropriately used in high level algorithms mainly due to the ease of programmability, wide range of commercial offerings, and low prices. With the improvement in speed of these processors, it is most likely that they will be continued to be used successfully for high-level vision tasks. On the other hand, some special architectures may be needed for some AI applications and rule-based systems [Kibl85, Tana86, Doug85, Wah86, Hwan87]. Since computers for AI applications relate mostly to non-vision problems, we will devote slightly less attention to them.

— Single instruction, multiple data stream (SIMD). In these systems, each operation is performed on many data items in parallel. Instructions are broadcast from a common controller to each processor in the architecture. There are several modes of SIMD processing, involving memory-addressing and communication. In general, massively parallel systems with fine-grained architectures require that memory addressing also be accomplished in SIMD mode. This implies that all processors have to address the same position in their local memory, which is the address broadcast by the central controller. It is important to note that SIMD communication also involves each processor choosing the same physical port to communicate to other neighboring processors. This distinction is relevant because it makes certain trivial operations more difficult to execute. For example, in an n-binary cube configuration operated in strict SIMD mode for communication, accessing the four 4-connected neighbors of each pixel may not be a constant-time operation.

Although SIMD instruction processing simplifies controllability and syncronization for fine-grained systems, SIMD memory-addressing largely complicates the programming of intermediate-level algorithms and the efficient manipulation of data structures. SIMD memory-addressing is needed as a consequence of the trade-off between chip pin-count and the number of on-chip processors. Also, there is another trade-off in the design of architectures: number of processors versus processor computing power. A machine with one hundred thousand processors has to be composed of bit-serial processing nodes. On the other hand, if only one thousand processors are integrated in a system, cost considerations allow for 16-bit and even 32-bit word processing nodes. In general, the issue of architecture-grain versus computing efficiency of individual processing elements is currently undergoing new thinking and controversy in the image community. Former designers of fine-arrays now advocate coarse-grained systems [Foun85].

Examples of SIMD machines include ILLIAC [McCo63], CLIP [Duff76], MPP [Fung77], GAPP [Davi84], DAP [Hunt81], and The Connection Machine [Hill85]. In the image community, most of the above SIMD machines have been explored only for image processing applications involving low-level or pixel-oriented transformations. Admittedly, the applicability of these architectures to window-based operators is direct and trivial. However, it is not unusual to see conceptual misunderstandings about what these machines can be expected to accomplish. For example, fine-grained mesh array architectures have optimal performance for neighborhood-based operations because the

5

complexity of algorithms scales only with the window size. This statement is often misunderstood to mean that array machines are unable to efficiently perform any other operation, including those arising in mid-level tasks or in symbolic computations. Local operations offer an optimal improvement over serial machines. In particular, the ratio "asymptotic complexity in a serial machine over number of processors in the array" is exactly the complexity of neighborhood-based operations (i.e., the number of pixels in the window). In practical terms, this statement remains valid only within some bounds. For example, the mesh processors are bit-serial, but many local operators need full 8-bit or 16-bit manipulation. In addition, the arithmetic and logic units cannot build a complete logic function with 9 inputs, so that all 3×3 non-linear morphology operators cannot be computed.

On the other hand, other operations such as histogramming or the Hough transform, are still possible to compute yielding significant asymptotic improvements over serial machines. Even connected component labeling is feasible with low demand on processing element hardware resources (such as the amount of local memory) as was recently shown in [Cyph87]. Asymptotically, all these mid-level operators have time complexity $O(N)$ for $N \times N$ mesh arrays. In general, much good research is going on in the area of parallel algorithms for SIMD machines and models. The output of some of this work is reflected in the existence of machines which support parallel versions of LISP, and the manipulation of non-iconic data structures [Hill85]. The treatment of vision algorithms in different parallel SIMD computers could well be the topic of a complete textbook. We will not elaborate on these issues any further, since they are beyond the scope of this book.
– Multiple instruction, single data stream (MISD). These architectures are also called pipelines, because multiple processing stages are cascaded to perform many operations on the same data stream. This classification in terms of "single data" is a bit incomplete because several different streams of data can actually exist in current pipelines. In some cases, the output of a stage can be fed recursively to the same stage. These multiple-stream machines are usually referred to as "parallel pipelines". "Single data" makes reference to the unique way data flow in the architecture, i.e., in raster or line-by-line mode. In this manner, data

flow through each stage of the pipeline where a certain operation is applied to a window of pixels. The very same definition of a pipeline brings about its major limitation: algorithms must be constrained to raster processing. Although this is a plus for several problems, i.e., some opertors can be efficiently implemented by visiting pixels in a raster format, it is a great disadvantage for many other algorithms which are not pipelineable. For example, rich data structures arising in most mid-level algorithms cannot be efficiently manipulated.

Pipelines can be classified as homogeneous or heterogeneous. Homogeneous pipelines are those in which all stages are identical. Examples of these are morphology machines, the WARP processor, the Radon transfrom architecture presented in this book, etc.. Heterogeneous pipelines include stages to perform different specific functions, such as histogramming, convolution, component labeling, etc.

Examples of current machines include the ERIM Cyto-computer [Ster79, Loug80], the CMU WARP processor [Gros85], the JPL programmable feature extractor [Gene85], MITE [Kimm85], etc. MISD architectures actually constitute the majority of commercial offerings due to their compatibility with the processing of serial video signals, relative ease of programming, and reasonable I/O capabilities. Their disadvantage is the limited speed improvement proportional to the number of pipeline stages. They are well suited to raster-based algorithms that find application both in window-based operations and, in particular, point-operators. Also, a few mid-level algorithms such as two-pass component labeling and feature extraction [Petk85] can be implemented by computing accessory information and intermediate data structures in conventional general-purpose microprocessors.

MISD machines appear to be the most successful solution to a number of specific machine vision applications. Also, they are the right approach for many algorithm-specific hardware implementations. The main reason for this success is their cost effectiveness and simple interconnection, allowing for systematic "plug-in" of new VLSI-based stages which also use raster-format data.

In this book, we will show a pipeline architecture for efficient implementation of the Radon transform and many other related operators.

– Multiple instruction, multiple data stream (MIMD). These architectures consist of several processors that apply different instructions to different data streams (i.e., they are real multiprocessors). Each processor has its own program memory and instruction-flow control. MIMD architectures potentially offer the highest speed improvement and versatility, but they still have many obstacles to overcome. The programming of these systems is not yet well-understood and the completely decentralized control presents synchronization problems. This is an area of very active recent research, and some commercial systems are starting to appear ("Cosmic Cube" [Seit85], Flexible Computing Flex [Ruet86], the NCUBE machine [NCUB], etc.). Among specific systems for machine vision, we can mention ZMOB [Rieg81] and PICAP [Anto81]. These architectures are best suited for high-level operations, where each processor may analyze a certain portion of the data (or image) or match different sets of rules.

High-level vision algorithms, as was remarked above, can be of numeric (traditional pattern recognition) or symbolic (AI-based) nature. While numeric problems are successfully solved using traditional computing machines (usually Von-Neuman with some number-crunching facilities), computers for AI are still in the research phase. AI machines pose new requirements like large memories, dynamic allocation, and interactive I/O, in order to support symbolic operations like search, pattern matching, selection, and sorting. Since AI architectures are also analyzed for many other non-vision algorithms, the reader is referred to [Wah86, Hwan87] for more information on the topic.

As was discussed earlier in this section, there are many other categories of machine vision architectures [Dani81]. For example, systems that allow for partitionable processor control have been studied. These systems consist of sets of processors operating in SIMD mode under different controllers. A reconfigurable machine has been proposed and a prototype built: PASM, where processors and controllers can be dynamically reconfigured [Sieg81]. These systems are called Multiple SIMD or SIMD-MIMD machines. There are other systems and proposed architectures that involve multiple control and different inter-processor communication. Most notable is an architecture suited to pyramid data structures [Uhr83]. This approach offers many interesting capabilities, such as ease of inter-node communication and efficient processing of multi-resolution data. This results in simple image processing at different levels of abstraction and/or resolution. These factors may be important for both low- and mid-level vision (edge detection, segmentation, and feature extraction). Paradigms for pyramid-machine algorithms are further described in [Tani87].

However, pyramid machines which have been attempted in hardware present a number of constraints. First, the fine-grained nature of the architectures restricts controllability to the SIMD mode of operation. At most, separate controllers could be provided for each layer of the pyramid. Also, the desired property of increasing processor communication bandwidth toward the apex has not yet been realized [Cant87, Meri87, Scha87]. Recent research studies on pyramids seem to indicate that low-level segmentation could be accomplished only in the presence of augmented pyramids by interleaving the nodes at different levels of the machine structure [Jain87]. These findings appear to be in agreement with the results reported in [Reev87], where it was shown that the additional hardware of conventional pyramid schemes offers little improvement in performance over planar mesh array architectures. In addition, interleaving pyramids and fat pyramids are more complex than the conventional pyramidal structure, and hence, they pose even more challenges for their hardware implementation.

It is clear that no single type of architecture is "best" when we consider the whole spectrum of operations (low-, mid-, and high-level). Therefore, the best combination depends on the particular machine vision application at hand, cost considerations, and speed and flexibility of the system.

With the rapid advance of hardware technology, and the ever-increasing demand for low-cost signal processing power, we see a proliferation of hardware building blocks and technologies available to the designer of machine vision systems. These building blocks may be divided into two categories: general-purpose components and special signal processing devices. The first category consists of various bit-slice processors, A/D converters and semi-custom digital devices (e.g., gate arrays, PALs). The latter category includes special signal processing microprocessors, image processing elements (e.g., cascadable convolvers) and special function units (e.g., the Bell Labs moment chip, AMI FFT chip).

It is very important to mention the role of VLSI technology and design tools, such as silicon compilers and other CAD tools. These developments will not only result in the repackaging of some older architectures, but will also open up many opportunities for mapping application-specific algorithms into VLSI in a relatively short time. The impact of VLSI lies not only in improving the cost/performance ratio, but also in opening up completely new avenues for exploring the design of architectures [Offe85, Ruet86, Cart86]. VLSI encourages different approaches to architecture design, favoring concurrency, proximity of memory and processors, regularity in data and control steps, regular and localized connections between processors, simple operations in many processors, minimization of I/O communications, etc. Image processing is well suited for these types of architectures. In fact, the major gains in VLSI-based solutions may result from the use of algorithms well-suited to this technology, rather than from the increase in speed and density of circuits.

1.2 The Radon Transform and the PPPE Architecture

The utilization of different representations for image data other than the usual pixel coordinate format is important for reducing the computational complexity of various algorithms in image processing and image analysis. The Radon transform [Helg80] provides one such representation, and is applicable to many image processing problems of both theoretical and practical interest. It not only holds the key for computer-aided tomography (CT) [Herm80], it also offers significant advantages for general image representation and manipulation [Breu75, Ma79, Pave78, Pavl78a, Wang75, Wu83, Yama78, Yee76].

Radon theory and the underlying mathematics are well-established for *deterministic functions* $f(x,y)$, and the applications are well known. They include CT applications in, for example, diagnostic medicine [Ravi79], radio astronomy [Brac79], electron microscopy [Gilb72b], optical interferometry [Swee73], and geophysical exploration [Deva84]. Other applications entail the reduction of complexity of algorithms, e.g., computing the 2-D Fourier transform in polar coordinates [Rose82], using the convolution theorem to reduce a projection of a 2-D convolution operation to a convolution of 1-D projections, etc.

Recently, extensions of Radon theory have been made to *random fields* [Jain84]. These are useful for filtering noise that has a statistical characterization from stochastic fields. In fact, it has been shown that for stationary fields, the projections are uncorrelated in orientation. Possible applications include filtering detector noise in CT reconstruction, and stochastic image filtering.

Projection space representation and manipulation of images have also been shown to have great impact on various machine vision problems. Within the realm of image analysis, algorithms have been developed to approximate the Hough transform along both linear *and* non-linear patterns, compute the convex hull and other geometric features of digital objects, generate multi-color polygonal masks for model-driven applications, and compute statistical features such as centroids and principal components of binary digital objects [Sanz87a, Sanz87b]. All these algorithms are presented in detail below.

Our goal is to provide an efficient engine for changing representations from image space to Radon space *and* back again, that is useful in all three of the above areas. This engine should permit the Radon transform and its inverse to be performed at high speeds, so that the power of the Radon space representation can be exploited for real-time computation in a variety of algorithms. We propose a powerful pipeline architecture, P^3E (Parallel Pipeline Projection Engine), that is a feasible hardware implementation of a discrete version of the projection operators (e.g., the Radon transform) and their inverses. We feel this pipeline is to the Radon transform what the FFT is to the Fourier transform, in terms of making Radon-based image processing and image analysis tractable (in this case by exploiting parallelism with an effective architecture).

The potential applications for P^3E are manifold. They include, for example: the discrete Radon transform, various machine vision applications, statistical filtering, backprojection, 2-D convolution, spectral estimation, computing the DFT in a polar raster, image coding, template matching, and graphics. P^3E has been shown to support the image analysis algorithms mentioned above under projection space representation and manipulation of images, and it has successfully been used in an automated visual inspection application (that of inspecting thin-film magnetic disk heads) [Petk85, Sanz86b].

Recently, we have been focusing on several image processing applications, all of which require the *back*projection of Radon data to obtain a resultant image [Hink87]. Our purpose has been to show the completeness of our model, i.e., show it is appropriate for obtaining a digital approximation not only to the Radon transform, but also to the *inverse* Radon transform. We have applied our pipeline to the problem of digital image reconstruction, using both non-iterative and iterative techniques, and using both digital projection data (collected using our pipeline) and sampled-continuous data (analogous to that collected in CT applications). We have experimented with 2-D convolution of an image with a kernel, which requires taking projections of the image and the kernel, convolving the individual 1-D projections at each orientation, and backprojecting the results. We have also investigated the use of our pipeline in such elementary graphics applications as rotation and translation of images, although we do not intend to compete with current state-of-the-art graphics techniques.

In this book, we survey some of our recent work on projection-based algorithms and architectures for machine vision. Specifically, we will consider the following features and operators for gray-level and binary images:

1. Projection data along linear patterns such as the parallel-beam configuration existing in computer aided tomography and spot-light mode synthetic aperture radar applications.
2. Projection data obtained along other general contours.
3. Convex hull approximations (and enclosing boxes), diameter, principal components, moments, etc.
4. Hough transforms for line and curve detection.
5. Polygonal and other multi-color masks for visual inspection, computer animation and other model-based applications.
6. Approximations to the inverse Radon transform.
7. Digital two-dimensional convolutions.
8. Reconstruction of simulated CT data.

9. Iterative reconstruction
10. Rotations and translations
11. Autocorrelations
12. DFT's in polar rasters

The above features and image operations, all of which are supported by P^3E, have been intensively studied and used in pattern recognition, computer vision, image analysis and image processing applications. However, the classical algorithms and digital architecture resources needed for the computation of many of these features are fairly disjoint. For example, known algorithms for computing the convex hull of an object are heavily oriented toward single-processor random-access architectures. On the other hand, techniques for computing polygonal binary and multi-colored masks require raster-scan logic and related architectural configurations. Furthermore, special purpose convolvers bear no relationship to the hardware resources necessary for either of these algorithms.

The undesirable characteristics of classical approaches for computing the above features that we would like to highlight are:

— The existing algorithms for the different problems appear very much unrelated to one another.

— The architectures that implement these algorithms require disjoint special-purpose hardware resources.
— The lack of parallelism, pipelining, or some other kind of multiprocessing affects the speed and performance of some of the current techniques.

Our approach to computing the above features and image operators provides a satisfactory solution to these three problems. It is based on a novel pipeline architecture that has a remarkable general purpose scope. To some extent, this architecture is composed of hardware resources that are extensions of components used in commercially available short-pipeline architectures [Uhr84]. Moreover, some of our algorithms can be implemented in conventional general purpose pipeline systems. Although this type of implementation does not yield fast algorithms as compared to our proposed architecture, it is extremely useful as a feasibility study, and constitutes a powerful tool for current practical applications of computer vision and image analysis. The reason for the importance of our algorithms in conventional general purpose pipeline systems is that past implementations of the above computations require the knowledge of pixel coordinates, or random access of the image memory, or special raster logic. Neither of the first two requirements can be met during processing cycles of commercially available general purpose pipeline architectures for image analysis. In addition, the raster logic necessary for certain feature extraction problems is seldom available as a part of existing configurations. We would like to emphasize that many of the traditional algorithms for computing the above features and image operators are neither well suited for parallel pipeline processing with (even lightly) general purpose image processing architectures, nor can they be subjected to modifications which make them suitable for some kind of efficient parallel computation.

The organization of this book is as follows. In Chap. 2, we present our model of digital projections, taken along linear contours, and our method for computing them. In Chap. 3 we discuss the architecture of P^3E, and describe its role in the real-time computation of projections. Chapter 4 covers the extension of P^3E to take projections along more general contours, which is useful in certain machine vision tasks. In Chap. 5 we discuss the application of our model to various image analysis problems in machine vision, and in Chap. 6 its application to various important image processing problems. We then present some recent results on Radon theory for random fields in Chap. 7. Finally, some applications of the algorithms to automated visual inspection problems are described in Chap. 8.

2. Model and Computation of Digital Projections

The parallel projection of a function $f(x,y)$ for a given angle θ is given by:

$$P_\theta(t) = \int_{L(\theta,\,t)} f(x,y)\, ds \qquad (2.1)$$

where $L(\theta, t)$ is a line at an angle θ with the y-axis and a distance t from the origin. Note that in terms of x and y, $t = x\cos\theta + y\sin\theta$. The two-dimensional function $P_\theta(t)$ is also the definition of the Radon transform of $f(x,y)$ [Helg80]. If we want to generate "digital" projection data, i.e., discrete projection data from a digital image I, we must consider a digital approximation to the Radon transform. We use the following:

$$P_\theta(t) \cong \sum_{(x_s,\,y_s)\,\in\, L_d(\theta,\,t)} f(x_s,y_s)\, \Delta_s \qquad (2.2)$$

where we are given samples $f(x_s,y_s)$ on a rectangular grid, Δ_s is the Euclidean distance between (x_s,y_s) and (x_{s-1},y_{s-1}), and $L_d(\theta, t)$ is a digital approximation to the line $L(\theta, t)$. We consider the $N \times N$ digital image I to be defined by $I(i,j) = f(j\delta, i\delta)$, where δ is the sampling distance between pixels in the x- and y-directions, and i and j are the integers $0, 1, 2, \ldots, N-1$.

Of course, there are many ways of digitally approximating the integral in (2.1), some of which require interpolation of the image to a denser grid, and some of which require the "weighting" of samples by a factor depending on the area of intersection between each pixel and an overlaid "thick" line. For example, in discrete models for CT [Herm80], the lines are defined as "beams" having a finite width τ, and only the area of each pixel covered by a given beam is integrated. With fast, real-time implementation in mind, such algorithmic complexities are to be avoided, especially since the computation in (2.2) is to be performed for many different t for each θ, and possibly for many different θ (depending upon the application).

An important attribute of the approximation in (2.2) is that no interpolation is required in image space to perform the computation. Furthermore, each pixel in the original image is visited only once, assuming we represent our digital lines in such a way that each pixel belongs to one, and only one, line. Nevertheless, the multiplication by Δ_s does represent a form of weighting for each pixel, since for each pixel s in a discrete line, Δ_s may be different. The most obvious way to avoid this weighting is to pull the Δ_s out of the summation in (2.2) by somehow defining a *common* Δ for all pixels along a given line such that:

$$\Delta_\theta(t) \cong \Delta_s \qquad \forall\ s \qquad\qquad (2.3)$$

for each line L_d at each orientation θ. Of course, by introducing such a simplification, we are introducing noise into our model. Noise considerations will be discussed later in Sect. 2.3. Now (2.2) becomes:

$$P_\theta(t) \cong \Delta_\theta(t) \sum_{(x_s, y_s)\, \in\, L_d(\theta,\, t)} f(x_s, y_s) \qquad\qquad (2.4)$$

For a given discrete line L_d, we define $\Delta_\theta(t)$ to be the reciprocal of the average number of pixels per unit length of the line, i.e.:

$$\Delta_\theta(t) = \begin{cases} \dfrac{l}{n-1} & n > 1 \\[2mm] 1 & n = 1 \end{cases} \qquad\qquad (2.5)$$

where l is the length of the digital line, or the Euclidean distance between the two end-point pixels in the line, and n is the total number of pixels contained within the line. Note that $\Delta_\theta(t)$ may vary from line to line at the same orientation. This point will be illustrated in the next section. Note also that $\Delta_\theta(t)$ may be precomputed for each line at a given orientation and stored for later use in the projection generation process.

Defining the "raw" projection data, i.e., the projection data before multiplication by $\Delta_\theta(t)$, as:

$$\tilde{P}_\theta(t) = \sum_{(x_s, y_s) \in L_d(\theta, t)} f(x_s, y_s) \tag{2.6}$$

and substituting into (2.4), we arrive at the following:

$$P_\theta(t) \cong \Delta_\theta(t)\tilde{P}_\theta(t) \tag{1}$$

A feasible algorithm to carry out the computation in (2.7) consists of the following two steps:

1. Obtain a digital representation of the contours L_d along which the projection $P_\theta(t)$ will be computed.
2. Compute $P_\theta(t)$ for the original image I utilizing the digital representation of the pattern obtained in Step 1.

Again with fast, real-time implementation in mind, we would like to tailor this algorithm so that the computation in (2.7) can be performed in a raster fashion. In this manner, we can avoid any random access of the image memory, and more importantly, we can attempt to map our model onto a pipeline architecture. To this end, we are confronted with two problems:

1. How to represent the digital lines L_d and
2. How to collect the projection data.

2.1 Representation of Digital Lines

As is well known, there exist several discrete representations of analog lines [Newm79], i.e., methods for digitally approximating L by L_d. For simplicity, we consider the case of representing families of parallel lines, along which we are collecting projection data (for generalization to other linear and non-linear patterns [Sanz87b], see Chap. 4). In the ensuing discussion, we will also refer to these lines as linear "contours" or "beams", since in the discrete case they are actually of finite width. For any orientation of the lines, we look for an image C_θ such that the set of pixels

$$L_d(\theta, k) = \{(i,j) : C_\theta(i,j) = k\} \tag{2.8}$$

is a *digital straight line* at orientation θ, for each value of k. Note that C_θ is itself a gray-level image. For linear contours, k will be a linear combination of the pixel coordinates i and j, i.e.:

$$k = \text{Round}[ai + bj + c] \qquad (2.9)$$

where the coefficients a and b depend only upon the orientation θ of the linear contours to be computed, a is equal to $b\tan\theta$, and c is some predetermined constant. In this case, the image C_θ will consist of a set of parallel digital lines, each with a different value of k. The choice of a and b scales the dynamic range of k, while the choice of c shifts the dynamic range. This computation is indeed suitable to raster mode processing, since the constants a, b, and c are predetermined for a contour image C_θ, and the calculation of k is performed on a pixel-by-pixel basis. i- and j-coordinate clocks can provide the values of i and j at each pixel.

As for the choice of coefficients, the trivial possibility is to use $a = \sin\theta$ and $b = \cos\theta$. The constant c should be chosen such that k is non-negative for all values of i and j, so that the image C_θ will be non-negative. For efficiency, one may wish to avoid floating- or fixed-point computation by approximating the terms ai and bj through table look-up operations (which is equivalent to rounding the products separately before adding them). The round-off error in this approach, of course, will result in some degradation in quality of the lines.

A second possibility is based on the following choice:

$$a = \begin{cases} 1 & \text{if } 45° < \theta \le 135° \\ \tan\theta & \text{otherwise} \end{cases}$$

$$b = \begin{cases} \dfrac{1}{\tan\theta} & \text{if } 45° < \theta \le 135° \\ 1 & \text{otherwise} \end{cases} \qquad (2.10)$$

The lines will now be formed by positive numbers with $c = 0$. More importantly, only one table look-up operation is required, and floating-point computation may be avoided with less error than before. It is interesting to remark that in this case, the computation of k may require a subsequent table look-up operation to compensate for the "compression" of the line pattern. Specifically, if the desired width of the lines (i.e., the "beam resolution") in the pattern is one pixel, then a post-multiplication by either $\cos\theta$ or $\sin\theta$ is needed, depending upon the orientation. However, if a table look-up operation is also used to approximate this post-multiplication, the propagation of round-off error will result in non-uniform line width.

Several examples are in order. Figure 2.1a shows the discrete pattern that approximates a family of parallel lines at an orientation of $\theta = 90°$ (for display purposes only, this and forthcoming contour images will be shown quantized to 5 bits, as in Fig. 2.1b, so that the nature of the "ramp" of gray levels is much more evident). This digital image is defined as follows:

$$C_{90}(i,j) = i \qquad \forall \text{ pixels } (i,j) \qquad (2.11)$$

As expected, the resulting image is such that for each gray level k, the set of pixels $\{(i,j):C_{90}(i,j) = k\}$ constitutes a digital straight line (in this particular case, a horizontal line).

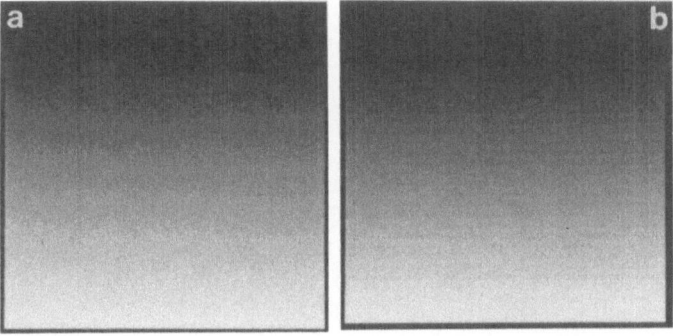

Fig. 2.1. Contour image for $\theta = 90°$ (a) and its 5-bit quantization (b)

Figures 2.2a,b show two more contour images for $\theta = 70°$ and $\theta = 130°$, respectively.

Figure 2.3 shows the $\Delta_\theta(t)$ array computed for lines at $\theta = 40°$. The fact that $\Delta_\theta(t)$ may vary from line to line at the same orientation is readily apparent from the figure, in which it ranges from a low value of 1.0 to

Fig. 2.2. Contour images for (a) $\theta = 70°$ and (b) $\theta = 130°$

a high of about 1.3. This variation demonstrates the importance of post-multiplying the raw projection data by Δ, particularly for reconstruction purposes. It is interesting to remark that there are orientations at which $\Delta_\theta(t)$ is constant for all lines, i.e., at $\theta = 0°$ and $\theta = 90°$.

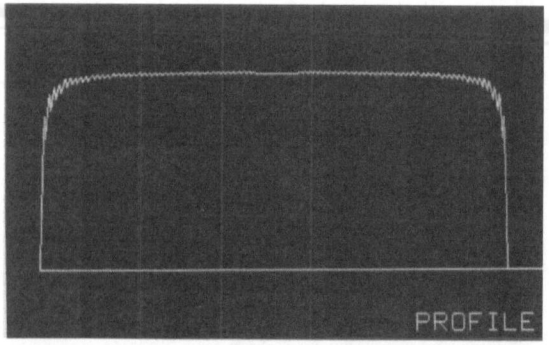

Fig. 2.3. The $\Delta_\theta(t)$ array for $\theta = 40°$ (the values range from 1.0 to 1.3)

Figures 2.4a-c show the effect of using different coefficients a and b in the computation of the linear-contour images, using (2.9) above, with $\theta = 40°$. Figure 2.4a shows a set of individual lines computed by using the first choice of coefficients given above, i.e., $a = \sin \theta$ and $b = \cos \theta$, and using table look-up operations to round the products in (2.9). The lines are located at regular intervals of 50 gray levels. They appear jagged in this case, due to the characteristics of the round-off error. Compare the quality of these lines with those in Fig. 2.4b, which were

20

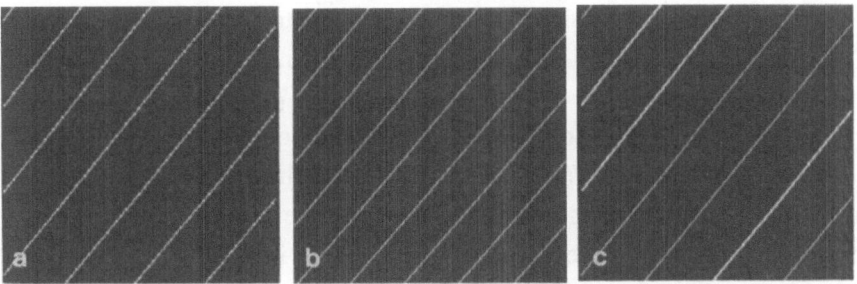

Fig. 2.4. Contour images for $\theta = 40°$ using different coefficients in (2.9): (a) $a = \sin\theta$ and $b = \cos\theta$, (b) $a = \tan\theta$ and $b = 1$, and (c) $a = \tan\theta$ and $b = 1$ followed by table-lookup decompression

obtained by using the coefficients given in (2.10). Again, table look-up was used instead of floating-point computation. Note that these lines are also separated by 50 gray levels, but they appear closer together due to the "compression" of the line pattern inherent in the choice of coefficients. Decompressing these lines by a subsequent table look-up operation, we obtain the new lines shown in Fig. 2.4c. As mentioned previously, due to the propagation of round-off error, the resulting lines are of non-uniform width. For further discussion of the quality of the lines and its relation to noise in the projection data, see Sect. 2.3.

2.2 Generation of Projection Data

Now that we have defined a representation for the linear contours, we turn to the problem of collecting projection data. Since $\Delta_\theta(t)$ enters the projection-taking process only as a post-multiplication, in this section we will focus on the problem of collecting the "raw" projection data, i.e., $\tilde{P}_\theta(t)$ as defined in (2.6). Collecting this data is equivalent to summing the pixel gray levels of an image I along a given set of projection contours. This process can be accomplished as follows. Given a digital image C_θ, which represents the family of projection contours, the projection of I along C_θ is given by:

$$\tilde{P}_\theta(k) = \sum_{\{(i,j):C_\theta(i,j)\,=\,k\}} I(i,j) \qquad (2.12)$$

In other words, if we consider the projection $\widetilde{P}_\theta$ to be a one-dimensional array, then for each pixel $I(i,j)$ in the original image, we use the value of the corresponding pixel in the contour image C_θ to address an element in the projection array, and we increment the contents of that element by the value of the pixel $I(i,j)$. After one pass through the image, which can be performed in a raster fashion, the complete projection of I along the parallel contours represented by the contour image C_θ will be stored in the array. The kth element in the array, i.e., $\widetilde{P}_\theta(k)$, will contain the summation of all pixel gray levels of I along the contour with value k in C_θ.

Collecting projection data in this manner is homologous to the operation of a gray-level histogrammer. Since it is performed on a pixel-by-pixel basis, completion of the contour image is not a necessary prerequisite for the projection-taking process. For each pixel (i,j), only the value of the contour image pixel (i,j), i.e., $C_\theta(i,j)$, need be computed. Consequently, the collection of projection data can be pipelined with the computation of the contour image, and the entire process demands only one raster pass through the image. Realistic applications may require projections at more than one orientation θ. In these cases, it is possible for projections at different orientations to be generated in parallel with each other, depending upon the available hardware. In the case where the original image I is a binary image, this procedure yields a pipeline implementation of the Hough transform for maximum likelihood line detection [Sanz87b]. For further discussion on parallelism and hardware architectures, see Chap. 3.

Figure 2.5a shows an image of an array of solder-ball shadows (shown as white blobs) overlaid on an integrated circuit die. These solder balls are used in the manufacturing and packaging of integrated circuits [Blan87]. For a first approximation to separating the individual solder-ball shadows, we take projections in several directions: $\theta = 0°, 90°, 45°$ and $135°$. Figure 2.5b shows the corresponding projection data obtained for $\theta = 0°$, i.e., collected along vertical linear contours. As is seen, the valleys between the main peaks of the projection indicate the most likely positions of separation between the individual columns of solder-ball shadows. In this manner, structural properties of the image can be determined through the use of projections. Another example is shown in Figs. 2.5c,d, which

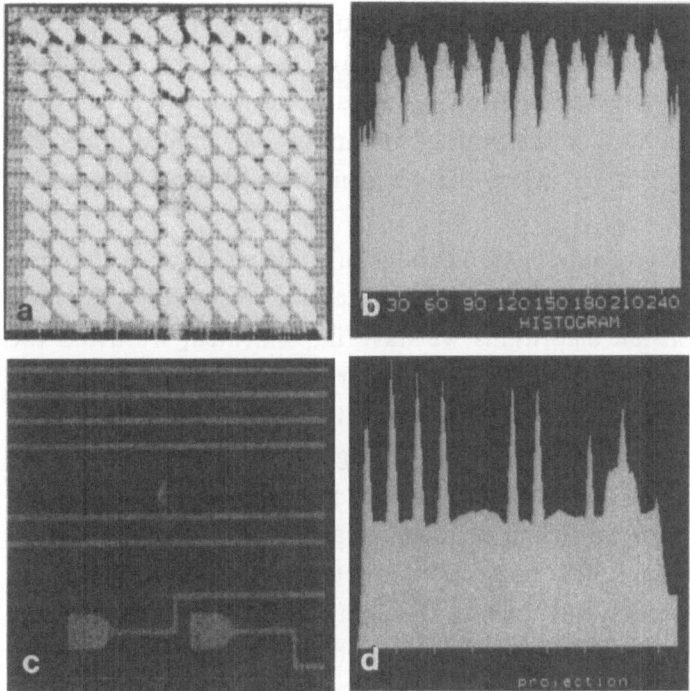

Fig. 2.5. Gray-level C4 image (a) with its projection data for $\theta = 0°$ (b), and gray-level PCB image (c) with its projection data for $\theta = 89°$ (d)

respectively show a typical printed circuit board image and its projection data for $\theta = 89°$. The peaks in this projection indicate the most likely positions of the horizontal conductor traces.

2.3 Noise Considerations

The coarseness of our approximation to the Radon transform provides us with the computational simplicity we need for efficient implementation. However, it also undermines the ability of our model to emulate a sampled-continuous analogue to the Radon transform. The noise inherent in our model arises from the relatively crude method of digitally approximating line integrals, and it is not only dependent on the orientation of the lines, but also on the data being projected. At $\theta = 0°$ and $90°$, for example, our digital lines are perfect one-pixel-wide discrete representations of their continuous counterparts. But, as the orientation approaches $\theta = 45°$ and 135°, the lines look more like ad hoc staircases, and the irregularity between lines at a given orientation becomes quite noticeable. This irregularity results in noise in the form of nonuniformly-sampled projection data, which may in turn affect the performance of image processing algorithms.

For many image analysis applications of projection-based representation and manipulation of images, this noise is not important. In fact, for the machine vision algorithms we have implemented, we avoid the multiplication by Δ altogether with no deleterious side effects. Examples of such applications include computing geometrical and statistical features of digital objects, performing boundary fitting and edge detection via the Hough transform, and generating multi-color polygonal masks for model-based applications. Nevertheless, for some image analysis and most image processing applications, this noise is undoubtedly important. First and foremost, these applications include those in which the image must be reconstructed from processed projection data (using non-iterative reconstruction techniques). Statistical filtering, 2-D convolution, CT reconstruction, and coding are all examples of these. Since the non-iterative reconstruction process is by nature very sensitive to high frequency noise, we would like to understand the noise-related effects of our model, and preferably compensate for them.

The well-known Shepp and Logan "head phantom" [Rose82], which is used for testing the accuracy of CT reconstruction algorithms, is shown in Fig. 2.6a as a 256 × 256 8-bit image. This image is comprised of ten ellipses, for which one may write analytical expressions for the projections. The projection of such an image is simply the sum of the projections of the individual ellipses. Proceeding in this manner, we can calculate exact sampled-continuous projection data at any orientation. Such data is shown in Fig. 2.6b for $\theta = 35°$. The corresponding digital projection data, collected using our model above with $a = \sin\theta$ and $b = \cos\theta$, is shown in Fig. 2.6c. The sampling period for both sets of data is the width of one pixel in the image. As can be seen, the digitally collected projection data is quite noisy. The positive frequencies in the 1024-element power spectrum of this noise are shown in Fig. 2.6d, with the origin on the left-hand side. The considerable high frequency content has a detrimental effect

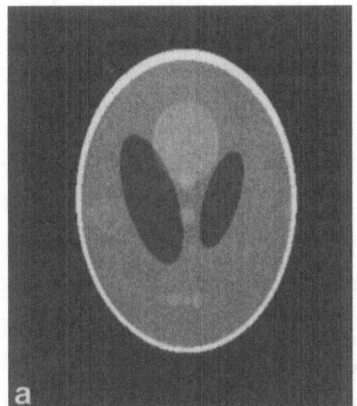

Fig. 2.6. Original Shepp and Logan "head phantom" image (a), with exact sampled-continuous (b) and digital projection data for $\Theta = 35°$ (c), power spectrum of noise in digital projection for $\Theta = 40°$ (d), and digital projection data using compressed contours for $\Theta = 35°$ (e)

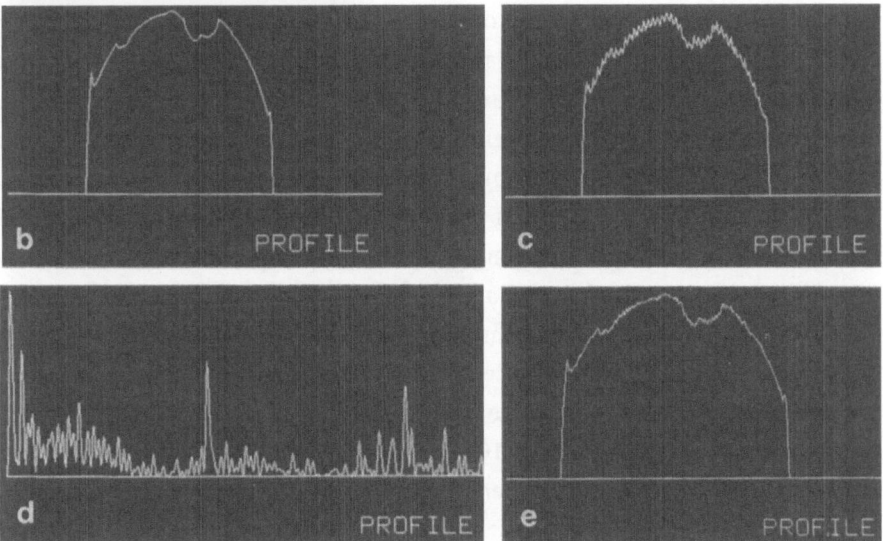

on the quality of any non-iterative reconstruction one may wish to perform. Numerous examples of such results will be shown later in Chap. 6.

To avoid the propagation of this high frequency noise in the process of reconstruction, several forms of compensation are practicable. First, since the noise is dependent upon orientation, one may try some form of orientation-dependent stochastic filtering using, for example, an optimal Wiener filter, as in [Jain84]. Second, one may filter the projections using a non-optimal bandlimiting window function. Examples of such functions are the Ram-Lak filter, the Shepp-Logan filter, the lowpass cosine filter,

25

and the generalized lowpass Hamming window (see Table 6.1 in Sect. 6.1). Of course, both methods result in a trade-off between image resolution and noise suppression. Finally, one may concentrate on enhancing the quality of the lines along which the projection data are collected. That is, we would like to use non-jagged lines of uniform width. For our model, the coefficients in (2.10) result in lines that appear to be of high quality (recall Fig. 2.4). Of utmost importance is the "compression" of the lines caused by these coefficients. This compression is non-linear with orientation, since it is a function of $\cos\theta$ or $\sin\theta$, and it facilitates the generation of lines of uniform width even as θ approaches 45° and 135°. Also, higher quality lines are possible without floating-point computation in this case, since only one term in (2.9) contributes to round-off error. Employing this alternate representation of the lines, the projection data obtained for the head phantom image at $\theta = 35°$ is shown in Fig. 2.6e. As is seen, there is a significant decrease in the amount of high frequency noise from the previous digital projection data (shown in Fig. 2.6c). The profile is wider than those shown in Figs. 2.6b,c, because the compression of the contours results in more data points.

In our experiments (see Chap. 6), we have implemented non-optimal filtering using the above bandlimiting window functions, and we have also tried two different representations for our contours: (1) using $a = \sin\theta$ and $b = \cos\theta$, which we will refer to as *representation I*; and (2) using the coefficients given in (2.10), which we will refer to as *representation II*. Optimal, orientation-dependent filtering is a subject of current research.

3. Architectures

As mentioned previously, the algorithms presented in Sects. 2.1 and 2.2 are suitable for pipeline processing. They may be implemented in either commercially available short-pipelines for image processing (e.g., those marketed by Gould, Vicom, Grinnel, etc.), or completely new pipeline architectures composed of both general- and special-purpose hardware components. Pipeline architectures are well known for their ease of interconnection [Kent85]. In this chapter, we concentrate on a new pipeline implementation for Radon-based image processing. However, other image-oriented architectures have been explored. Particularly appealing are the MIMD/SIMD approaches considered in [Rice85] and [Silb85], M/SIMD machines [Ibra85], and systolic networks [Hara85], among many others.

The implementation of our algorithms in commercially available short-pipelines is straightforward for binary images (see Sect. 3.5), and is discussed in detail in [Sanz87b].[1] A major problem with these pipelines is that they provide only a single-stage pipe, and thus eliminate the possibility of pipelining the projection generation process for more than one orientation at a time. Furthermore, they do not provide the flexibility necessary to pipeline contour image generation with projection data collection in a single pass through the image. Therefore, two passes are required to generate projection data at each orientation: one to generate the contour image and one to collect the projection data.

To avoid these problems, we turn to the second alternative, that of developing a new pipeline architecture based on both general- and special-purpose hardware components. We would like a single stage in our

---

1 The reason for constraining the applicability of commercial pipelines to binary images is that most have histogrammers that do not support gray-level increments.

pipeline to be capable of taking a projection at a programmed orientation, using only one pass through the image. Then, by pipelining many stages together, we will be able to take projections at many different orientations in a single pass through the image. Each stage should contain the following components:

1. contour image generator
2. projection data collector
3. additional components for control and added flexibility

3.1 The Contour Image Generator

The contour image generator (CIG) may be designed in one of two ways: (1) with relatively simple off-the-shelf hardware; or (2) as a custom-made chip. Both alternatives are feasible, and both have unique advantages and disadvantages.

In choice (1), floating-point hardware would be cumbersome, especially for ambitious throughput rates. The CIG would thus require substantial amounts of look-up table (LUT) memory to perform the necessary operations, as mentioned in Sect. 1.1. The actual amount of memory would depend on the dynamic range required for the contour image and intermediate computations [Sanz87b]. In this form, the CIG would require more preprogamming overhead, but it would also handle high throughput rates with a high degree of generality. Both linear *and* non-linear contour patterns would be possible, simply by reloading the LUT's.

One such potential configuration is shown in Fig. 3.1. In this design, the i and j coordinates of each image pixel are provided by the clocks C_i and C_j, and are fed through two LUT's to the arithmetic unit (AU). The function of the LUT's is to perform the multiplications ai and bj, which are inputs to the AU. The CIG then performs the linear operation $ai + bj + c$, as in (2.9). As mentioned above, it is interesting to note that non-linear functions of the i and j coordinates may also be computed by these LUT's, thus allowing the generation of curved patterns. Finally, the output of the CIG is passed through another LUT, which is used to scale and quantize the contour image pattern. Each computed contour image pixel is then sent over a dedicated bus to the projection data collector.

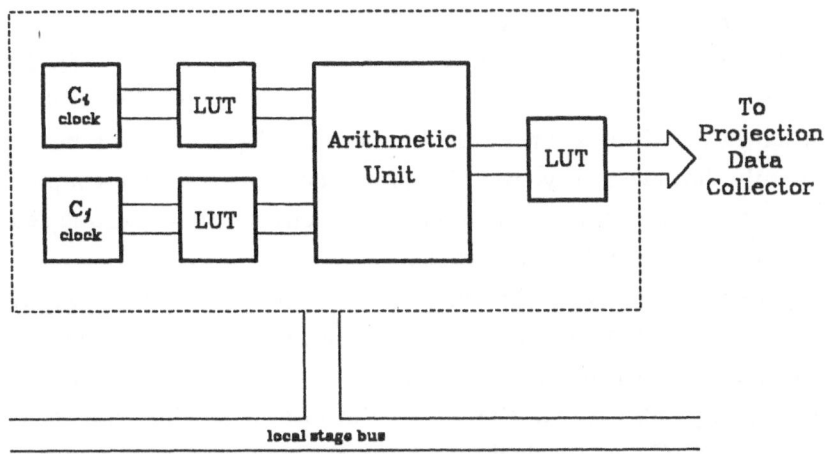

Fig. 3.1. Contour image generator

The design of a CIG chip, as in choice (2), would most likely incorporate floating- or fixed-point computation on the chip to eliminate the otherwise unwieldy LUT memory requirements. Simple arithmetic operations would be available to implement (2.9) directly. Provisions could be made for generation of certain classes of more complex patterns, e.g., second-order non-linear patterns. However, the range of possible patterns would be constrained by the available operations, and the complexity of the possible operations would be constrained by the desired throughput. In other words, the generality of the LUT approach would be lost. Looking at the bright side, such flexibility is unnecessary for most applications. One real advantage of this approach is that the preprogramming overhead would be kept to a minimum, and would simply consist of loading a few registers. Other advantages include those benefits inherent in chip customization: compactness, speed, and efficiency.

3.2 The Projection Data Collector

The projection data collector (PDC) is equivalent to a gray-level hardware histogrammer with an address space capable of handling the range of contour values. With $N \times N$ images and linear contours, the number of possible contour values does not exceed $2N$. Thus, in this case, the number of necessary address bits in the histogrammer is $\log_2(2N)$. If $N = 512$, the number of required bits is 10. Currently, to our knowledge, all such hardware histogrammers on the market exist only at the board level (recently, however, gray-level histogrammer chips with fewer inputs have been designed). For compactness and efficiency, a customized histogrammer chip would be preferable.

To illustrate the use of the PDC, let us suppose that the original image I and the contour image C are fed to a hardware histogrammer. Note that I is passed from the previous stage over the external pipeline bus, and subsequently to the PDC over the local stage bus, and C is passed from the CIG over the dedicated CIG-PDC bus. The histogrammer has a set of registers that are addressed by the pixel gray-levels of C. It is programmed to increment the contents of the register $C(i,j)$ by the value of $I(i,j)$. If $R[i]$ denotes the ith register of the histogrammer, and $\{R[i]\}$ denotes the contents of $R[i]$, then the function performed for each pixel (i,j) is:

$$\{R[C(i,j)]\} = \{R[C(i,j)]\} + I(i,j) \tag{3.1}$$

Equation (3.1) shows that the histogrammer operates on only one pixel at a time, which confirms the previous assertion that this operation may be pipelined with the computation of the contour image C. As a result, there is *no* need to store the contour image that is generated. A contour image pixel is generated, used to update the corresponding projection data in the histogrammer, and discarded. Storing these images would be a major drawback due to the large number of bits per pixel.

Note that this operation does not incorporate the multiplication by Δ. Many algorithms, especially those in image analysis applications, do not suffer performance degradation from the omission of this multiplication, and thus we leave it as optional. The applications that do require the multiplication mainly involve algorithms for non-iterative image reconstruction, and algorithms for frequency-domain estimation. In these cases, as will be seen below, it is necessary to perform additional signal processing on the raw projections. For this reason, we differentiate between projection data collection and Δ multiplication, and associate the latter with the signal processing portion of the stage (as described in the next section).

30

3.3 Additional Hardware

Additional hardware is necessary in each pipeline stage for added flexibility and control. First, we would like the same pipeline to support not only the projection process, but also the *back*projection process, i.e., the inverse projection operation. In other words, we want the same hardware to be useful for both projection *and* reconstruction. In Sect. 6.1 we will describe the backprojection operation in detail. For now, it suffices to say that in non-iterative reconstruction, intermediate signal processing on the projection data is necessary for backprojection. Thus, it is desirable to include a 1-D signal processing chip in each stage. Several such chips are currently available on the market. An important ramification of backprojection is that fixed- or floating-point processing of projection data becomes necessary, because of the Δ multiplication, the additional signal processing, and the way in which the data is recombined at each pixel to reconstruct the image.

Second, for various algorithms in image analysis, it is advisable to have both a general-purpose LUT in each stage, and an ALU to perform simple arithmetic and logical operations on the incoming image pixels. The LUT is useful for thresholding projection data, and the ALU is useful for combining incoming pixels with internal results at each stage, with the ultimate purpose of creating output images according to the application. These two components are useful in certain image analysis applications, such as computing classical geometric features of digital objects, and generating multi-color polygonal masks [Sanz87b]. The ALU is *also* necessary for reconstruction, which requires it to have fixed- or floating-point functionality, as mentioned above.

Finally, control and interface logic are requisite for operation, and a moderate amount of local memory is needed for storing constants (e.g., the Δ array for a given orientation) and intermediate results. The control of the stage is relatively simple. For example, to take projections of an image, each stage in the pipe would be configured for a certain orientation. In this case, the orientation would affect only the operation of the CIG. During execution, as each image pixel is read from the external pipeline bus and fed to the PDC, the corresponding contour image pixel is generated by the CIG, and also fed to the PDC. The PDC then increments the appropriate register, and the original image pixel is sent out to the next stage in the pipeline. After one pass through the image, the PDC histogrammer in each stage contains the complete projection for the given orientation. The operation of the pipeline during reconstruction will be described in Sect. 6.1. For a description of the operation of the pipeline in several image analysis applications, refer to Chaps. 5 and 6.

3.4 Putting It All Together: P^{3}E

An individual stage is shown in Fig. 3.2. To recapitulate, each stage consists of the following components: a CIG, a PDC, a signal processing chip, a general-purpose LUT, an ALU, some local memory, and the control and interface logic. The stages are pipelined together via the external P^{3}E bus connections, and the host computer has access to each individual stage via the host control and data bus connection (for preprogamming, extracting projection data, etc.).

The complete P^{3}E pipeline is shown in Fig. 3.3. There are many praiseworthy features of this architecture:

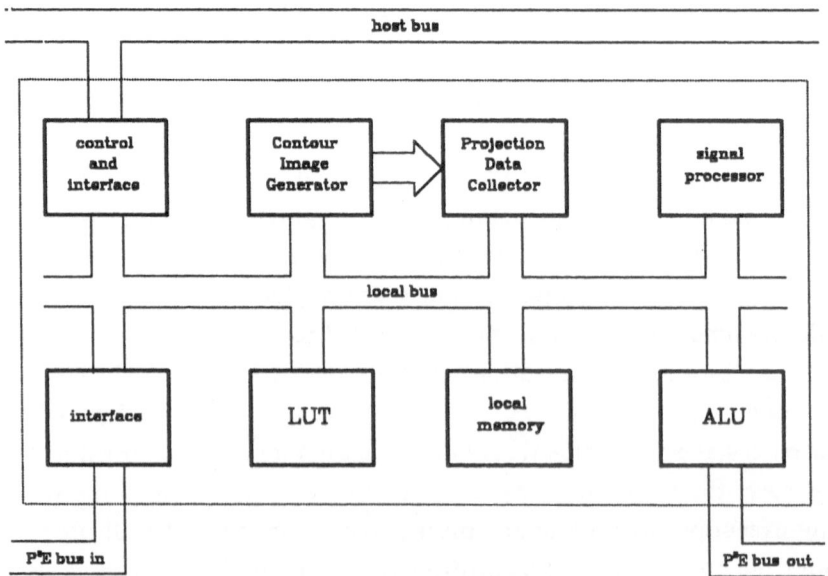

Fig. 3.2. Individual P^{3}E stage

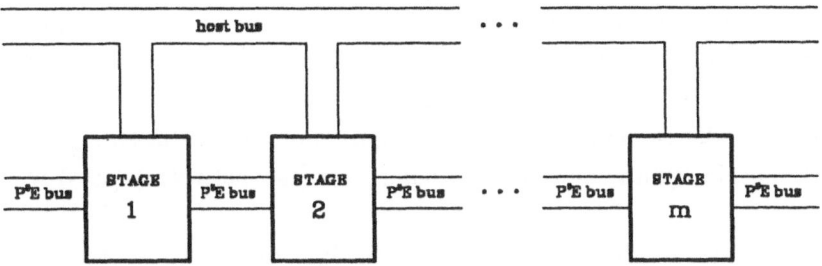

Fig. 3.3. Complete P³E pipeline

— The architecture supports real-time projection-based image processing and image analysis.

— The architecture remains the same for both deterministic and stochastic Radon transform applications, in addition to applications involving projection-space representation and manipulation of images.

— The building blocks are simple, and complicated software is not required.

— The architecture is extremely decoupled, with no complex global interconnections or computations.

— The architecture exhibits a high degree of replication, and is amenable to VLSI implementation.

— Any level of parallelism may be added simply by adding stages.

— The architecture scales easily with image size.

The last point merits elaboration. The complexity of the histogramming function is $O(n)$, where n is the number of incoming data points. Since there is a constant amount of processing per pixel, the architecture can maintain the same throughput rate without requiring additional speedup. The only hardware change required with increasing image size is a logarithmic increase in the size of the PDC histogrammer. Also, in reconstruction applications, one may wish to use projections at more orientations as the image size increases. Our architecture can handle more projections in one of two ways. First, and most obviously, additional stages may be added to the pipeline to handle each additional orientation.

Second, one may simply make more than one pass through the pipe, storing intermediate results after each pass. In fact, this is true for any application. For example, in an application where 12 projections are required, and the available pipeline is composed of only 4 stages, 3 passes through the pipe (with some data transfer overhead between passes) will do the job.

As a final architectural note, the pipeline above is not the only feasible configuration. The stages may be placed in parallel with one another in a multiple data-stream configuration, and the results combined via a multiplexed ALU to produce a single output stream. Although one gains in overall execution speed by eliminating the pipeline propagation delay, one loses in architectural flexibility. That is, the architecture is not as decoupled, because the front-end to the output ALU circuitry would be difficult to modify for additional stages. For this reason, we prefer the pipeline configuration of P^3E.

3.5 Implementation in Commercially Available Pipelines

In commercially available short-pipeline image processors (such as DeAnza, Grinnel, IBM 7350, Vicom, etc.), one can perform a number of operations on digital images in a fraction of a second. Typical manipulation of images in these architectures consists of performing table look-up, two-dimensional convolution, histogramming, and logical and arithmetic operations among several images. In architectures whose processor pass is performed at video rate, these operations can be pipelined and executed on 512×512 images in 1/30 of a second. Given that P^3E is not yet available, one would like to implement projection-based algorithms in commercially available pipelines.

Since these pipelines are based on raster-mode processing, and do not allow random access of the image memory during a processor pass, it is desirable to use the same general approach as described above, with some minor implementation modifications. Thus, we would like to be able to generate a contour image and use that to address a histogrammer. In commercially available systems, histogrammers usually operate on two images, and in some processors the histogrammed image I has to be binary (called the "mask"). In this case, the histogramming function is referred to as "masked histogramming", since the counting is activated only when $I(i,j)$ is not zero, and the increment for the corresponding register is always 1. Since commercially available pipelines do not directly support data-dependent increments during histogramming, implementing projection operators for gray-level images is very inefficient (though not impossible). This lack of support motivates the design of special hardware to augment the histogramming facilities of such pipelines.

The problem of generating the contour image is also somewhat dependent on the particular pipeline. In the DeAnza image processing system, for example, a hardware table can be addressed by using either the x or y coordinate of an image buffer, but not both, in a single processor pass. Therefore, it is possible to generate a horizontal (or vertical) ramp in one image processor pass. In some other systems, like the IBM 7350, an image can be transposed in one pass, thus if a horizontal ramp is available, a vertical ramp can be produced as its transpose in one processor pass. These hardware facilities are not enough to generate a contour image C_θ at an arbitrary orientation θ in a direct way. However, C_θ can be efficiently computed by means of an indirect procedure which is suitable for any general purpose image processing architecture. The key property is that any ramp C_θ is a linear combination of a vertical and horizontal gray-level contour image:

$$C_\theta(i,j) = aC_0(i,j) + bC_{90}(i,j) \qquad \text{for all pixels } (i,j) \qquad (3.2)$$

In other words, the gray-level contour images C_0 and $C_{90} = C_0'$ are enough to obtain any other contour image by a suitable pixel-by-pixel linear combination of these two images, where the coefficients a and b depend only on the slope $\tan \theta$ of the contour image to be computed. Note that this method uses C_0 and C_{90} to provide the i and j coordinates of the image, and these two contour images need to be stored in image planes so that they can be fed to the arithmetic processor. Using this method requires either one or two processor passes to generate an arbitrary contour image C_θ, depending upon the available architecture.

The above methods have been successfully used for mapping our model of digital projections onto a particular commercially available short pipeline, to implement various image analysis tasks. This implementation is currently being used in the automatic visual inspection of magnetic thin-film disk heads [Sanz86b], and is described in detail in Chap. 8.

4. Projections Along General Contours

The powerful CIG in Fig. 3.1 can also be used to generate ramps which are not linear, along with other more sophisticated patterns. For example, the operation $\sqrt{c_1(i - i_1)^2 + c_2(j - j_1)^2}$, where c_1, c_2, i_1, and j_1 are constants, is suitable for generating elliptical ramps, and is specifically useful for drawing circular multi-tone masks (see Sects. 5.4 and 5.5). Another example is the operation $c\sqrt{ij}$, where c is a constant, which yields hyperbolic ramps.[2] In this case, it is necessary that the CIG be capable of taking integer products between the image coordinates.

Figure 4.1a shows a circular coordinate-reference image where the center of the pattern is at the center of the image. On the other hand, Figs. 4.1b,c show elliptical ramps obtained by different choices of the parameters i_1, j_1, c_1, and c_2. Also, Fig. 4.1d shows a hyperbolic ramp. The square root computation necessary in these patterns may require elaborate hardware. However, a simple way to implement this square root is by table look-up. Moreover, it is interesting to remark that for elliptical patterns which are not rotated (such as that shown in Fig. 4.1b), the CIG in Fig. 3.1 does not need to take products. The reason is that the required operations can be performed by using look-up tables. For example, if a circle with center at (i_1, j_1) is desired, the image coordinates i and j can be fed to the look-up tables which are loaded with the functions $(i - i_1)^2$ and $(j - j_1)^2$. The output look-up table is predefined with a rounded square root function. An analogous approach can be followed to compute ellipses (if rotation is necessary then products between image coordinates are unavoidable). Also, other more sophisticated linear patterns can be generated. An example is the classical fan-beam arising

---

2 Hyperbolic ramps are useful for computing principal components of binary objects, as will be shown later in Sect. 5.1.

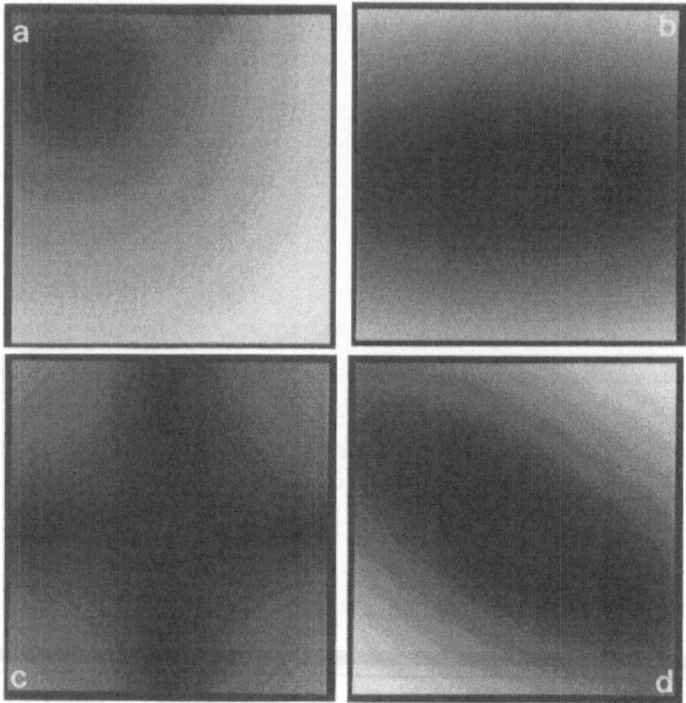

Fig. 4.1. More general types of contour images: (a) circular, (b),(c) elliptical, and (d) hyperbolic

in tomographic applications. The form of certain fan-beam coordinate-reference images is given by $FB(x,y) = (y + d) / (x + e)$, where d and e are constants.

The number of gray levels necessary for generating the patterns shown above is much larger than that of the parallel-line case of Sect. 2.1. For the circular patterns, the number of gray levels is (assuming c_1 and c_2 not greater than 1) at most $2N^2$, for an $N \times N$ image. For the hyperbolic ramps, the number is N^2. In the case of $N = 512$, this means that we should be able to design tables (and/or histogrammers) with 2^{19} entries. On the other hand, it is also clear that at the expense of losing some resolution in the pattern, a linear scale factor may reduce the dynamic range of the gray levels, i.e., $c = c_1 = c_2 = $ constant less than 1.

Another possibility is to have a few base-limit registers for slicing a gray-level ramp image. These registers have a number of different uses, and constitute a reasonable alternative to cope with the excessively large dynamic ranges of these algebraic patterns in general purpose systems. For example, let us denote by B_1 and L_1 a base and limit register, respectively. The function to be performed can be described as follows. If the current pixel value is within the range of values specified by B_1 and L_1 then subtract a certain amount given by a register A_1 from the pixel value; in any other case, reset the pixel value to a predetermined number. Note that the definition of the values of the registers B_1, L_1 and A_1 is left to the user. However, it is clear that for efficient use of this slicing facility, B_1 and L_1 should be chosen such that $L_1 - B_1$ equals the number of registers in the histogrammer or entries in the look-up tables. In addition, register A_1 is used to shift the pixel value within the range of feasible addresses for the histogrammer or look-up table.

A certain choice of the base and limit registers indicates which "slice" of the coordinate-reference image has to be used for the histogramming or other table look-up operations. After this step is completed and the partial projection obtained in the histogrammer's registers is stored in the host computer, we should continue the process by offsetting the base and limit registers by M and trying the same procedure again. As is seen from (4.2) below, this should be repeated as many times as the ratio

$$N_T = \frac{N_g}{M} \tag{4.1}$$

indicates, where N_g is the total number of gray levels in the ramp image. It is desired that N_T not be too large, so that the projection operation can be completed in a few passes through the hardware configuration.

A more problem-oriented solution which is an efficient implementation of the base-limit registers facility described above is as follows. Let us split the bit configuration of a pixel into an upper part and a lower part. The number of bits corresponding to the lower part N_{lg} should be in correspondence with the number of addressable registers in the histogrammers or the number of entries in the look-up tables (in other words, the number of entries or registers M should equal $2^{N_{lg}}$). The upper-part bits of a pixel are used to decide which of two possible tags the pixel will be given. These tags indicate whether the pixel is to be used or ignored in any further processing. In particular, for taking projections, the histogrammer should ignore (i.e., not use in the histogramming) those pixels which have some predefined tag.

As in the base-limit register approach, we would like to classify each pixel as belonging to one of the following intervals of gray levels:

$$(0, M - 1), (M, 2M - 1), \dots, [\,(\frac{N_g}{M} - 1) * M, N_g - 1\,]\qquad(4.2)$$

It is clear that the decision as to which of these intervals a pixel value belongs can be made by using the upper part bits only. A register of at least $\log_2(N_g / M)$ bits should be provided, so that the bit configuration corresponding to the projection slice to be computed can be loaded by the user.

The advantages of this later approach are as follows.

– The classification of each pixel (i.e., whether it belongs to the selected slice of the coordinate-reference image or not) is made by checking a few bits (i.e., the upper-part $\log_2(N_T)$ bits). Therefore, the process of tagging pixels is very fast.
– No arithmetic operation is necessary since the lower-part bits of a tagged pixel constitute the correct address for further processing.

As an example, let us consider the circular pattern given in Fig. 4.1a. Since the image size is $N = 512$, the number of gray levels in the pattern is not more than 2^{19}. Assuming that our histogrammers have 2^{17} registers, we will need four different slices to compute the projection data.

Fig. 4.2. Slices for reducing dynamic range

The location of the slices in the coordinate-reference image are shown in Fig. 4.2.

Certainly, some other alternatives are possible for generation of the above contour images. For example, a package of graphics routines can be used to draw all the curves in a pattern. Every time a curve is drawn, a new code is assigned. The disadvantages of this approach are rather evident. Filling the image with contours requires quite a bit of execution time and the processing (which is typically accomplished by using random access in the image plane) is not well-suited for pipelining or some other kind of parallelism. On the other hand, the graphics approach may be reasonable if the aesthetic appearance of the patterns is relevant. Certainly, this is not the case of the problems addressed in this manuscript.

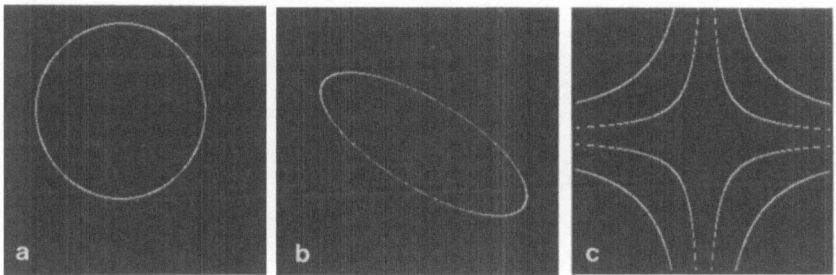

Fig. 4.3. Curves generated by look-up table operation applied to ramp images

However, the question of whether or not the prescribed technique is suitable for graphics purposes can be raised. We believe that if drawings of isolated contours are desired, the approach presented above is not a good one for graphics applications. As an example, we show in Fig. 4.3 a set of rotated ellipses and circles obtained by using the corresponding non-linear ramps and thresholding the resulting images (a pipelined operation performed by hardware table look-up). As is clearly seen, the quality of the drawings is inferior compared to that obtained by using current graphics facilitites. On the other hand, our approach may be very useful for patterns in which fine detail is not needed. For example, the thick lines of Fig. 2.4, and the circular slices of Fig. 4.1 are interesting cases. A particular application of this approach is to "filling regions from contour data" in a completely pipelined mode. We will return to this subject in Sects. 5.3-5.

5. P^{3}E-Based Image Analysis Algorithms and Techniques

P^{3}E-based algorithms have been developed for various important image analysis tasks in the realm of projection-space image representation and manipulation. The developed algorithms include computing classical statistical and geometrical features of digital objects, approximating the Hough transform for detecting the maximum-likelihood position of linear and non-linear edges, and generating multi-color polygonal masks for model-based applications. The purpose of this chapter is to explain these algorithms in detail, and present experimental results illustrating their performance.

5.1 Computing Convex Hulls, Diameters, Enclosing Boxes, Principal Components, and Related Features

Finding the convex hull of digital objects is an important problem in pattern analysis and classification. There are many algorithms for constructing the convex hull of a two-dimensional set of points under particular assumptions [Skla72, Skla82, Tous83]. On the other hand, for an unstructured set of n points the worst-case complexity of the problem is $O(n \log n)$. Several algorithms are known to have this complexity [Akl79, Bhat83]. Other procedures run with linear average complexity [Devr81, Eddy77].

In this section, the problem of finding the convex hull of a digital two-dimensional blob is revisited, and an algorithm is presented which computes approximated convex hulls. This technique can be implemented efficiently in general purpose image processing architectures. For more discussion and comparisons between our technique and classical approaches the reader is referred to [Sanz87b].

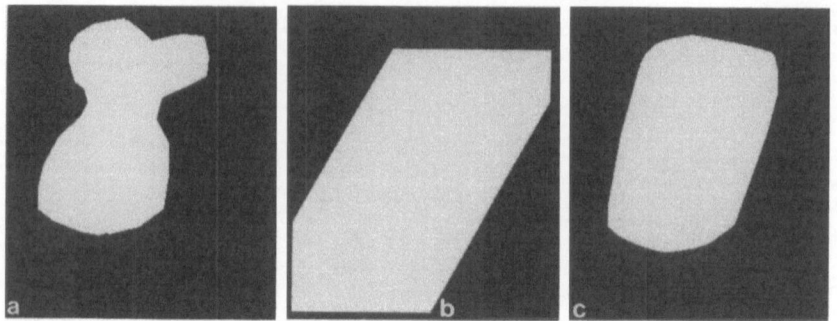

Fig. 5.1. (a) Digital blob, (b) binary band at $\theta = 30°$, and (c) convex hull approximation

Let us suppose that B is a blob in a $N \times N$ digital image (see Fig. 5.1a).

The convex hull of B is the smallest convex set which contains B.[3] Equivalently, the convex hull CH_B of B is the intersection of all semiplanes containing B as a subset. In the latter property, there is a certain redundancy. For any given orientation θ, it is necessary to use only two semiplanes which are determined by the points $P_\theta = (x_{min}, y_{min})$ and $Q_\theta = (x_{max}, y_{max})$ such that

$$
\begin{aligned}
C_{min}(\theta) &= \min\{x\cos\theta + y\sin\theta, (x,y) \in B\} \\
&= x_{min}\cos\theta + y_{min}\sin\theta
\end{aligned}
\tag{5.1}
$$

$$
\begin{aligned}
C_{max}(\theta) &= \max\{x\cos\theta + y\sin\theta, (x,y) \in B\} \\
&= x_{max}\cos\theta + y_{max}\sin\theta
\end{aligned}
\tag{5.2}
$$

The points P_θ and Q_θ (which may not be uniquely determined by the properties (5.1,2)) are extreme points of the digital object B in the direction given by the angle θ. It is now clear that the blob B is contained in the band

$$
BAN(\theta) = \{(x,y) : C_{min}(\theta) \le x\cos\theta + y\sin\theta \le C_{max}(\theta)\}
\tag{5.3}
$$

---

3 We do not make any attempt here to discuss the transition between continuous and discrete convexity. The reader is referred to some excellent papers in [Skla72, Kim82, Kim81, Skla70], among others.

Moreover, CH_B is now given by the intersection of $BAN(\theta)$'s for $0 \le \theta < 180$, i.e.,

$$CB = \bigcap_{0 \le \theta < 180} BAN(\theta) \qquad (5.4)$$

It is recognized that the computation of P_0, P_{90}, Q_0, and Q_{90} (i.e., the extreme points of the object in the x and y directions) is the first step of a well-known algorithm for finding the convex hull of a set of n points whose complexity is $O(n \log n)$ [Bhat83]. Note that in (5.4), on the contrary, it is not required to know P_0, Q_0, P_{90}, and Q_{90}, but $C_{min}(0)$, $C_{max}(0)$, $C_{min}(90)$, and $C_{max}(90)$ instead.

If a finite set of angles $\theta_1, \theta_2, \dots, \theta_k$ is chosen, then

$$\hat{CH}_B = \bigcap_{i=1}^{k} BAN(\theta_i) \qquad (5.5)$$

is an approximation of the convex hull CH_B.[4] This section shows an algorithm based on (5.5) for computing the convex hull, diameter and other features of digital objects such that:

— It is easily supported by P^3E (it can also be efficiently implemented in general purpose image processing architectures), and its complexity is independent of the number of points of the digital blob B.

— It does not require random access of the image memory.

— It does not require manipulation of additional data structures for solving the problem.

— It produces the approximated convex hull $\hat{CH}_B$ in the form of a digital image which is very suitable for further image analysis (without needing additional conversions between different data representation schemes).

---

4 There is nothing novel in the use of this approximation for convex hull computations since formula (5.4) is well known from the early days of convex functional analysis.

The procedure can be divided into the following two steps:

1. Efficient computation of $C_{min}(\theta)$ and $C_{max}(\theta)$ for all $\theta = \theta_1, \theta_2, \ldots, \theta_k$

2. Efficient image representation of $BAN(\theta)$ for $\theta = \theta_1, \theta_2, \ldots, \theta_k$

In Chaps. 2 and 3, P^3E was shown to obtain linear mass distributions (projections) along any direction θ based on coordinate-reference images (ramps) and histogrammers. The first non-zero entry of the histogram corresponds to $C_{min}(\theta)$ as defined in (5.1). Similarly, $C_{max}(\theta)$ is the last non-zero entry of the histogram. If the space of possible angles is quantized into $k = 90$ different angles (i.e., at an interval of 2 degrees if the quantization is uniform), the generation of all the gray-level ramps and the corresponding histograms would take a few seconds (about 5 seconds in some of the commercially available systems). Certainly, this time can be dramatically reduced by designing a parallel general purpose image processing architecture.

As is clearly seen, $C_{min}(\theta)$ and $C_{max}(\theta)$ can be efficiently computed for all $\theta = \theta_1, \ldots, \theta_k$. However, the question of how to *represent* and *use* the band $BAN(\theta)$ defined in (5.3) remains, at this point, unanswered. We will next show that the gray-level ramps and some simple general purpose image processing hardware provide an elegant and efficient solution to this problem.

Consider the parallel-line ramp C_θ for a certain direction θ. The numbers $C_{min}(\theta)$ and $C_{max}(\theta)$ are obtained from the directional mass histogram (i.e., the projection). The band $BAN(\theta)$ can be represented as a *binary image* by passing the image C_θ through a look-up table predefined with the following function:

$$T(g) = \begin{cases} 1 \, , & \text{if } C_{min}(\theta) \leq g \leq C_{max}(\theta) \\ 0 \, , & \text{otherwise} \end{cases} \tag{5.6}$$

It is easily seen that the operation implemented by this look-up table is a simple thresholding whose output image $T(C_\theta)$ defines the digital band $BAN(\theta)$. Figure 5.1b illustrates a band obtained by this process for a certain angle. After the image $BAN(\theta_i)$ is obtained for a certain i, it should also be used to update the convex hull approximation by performing the following intersection:

$$\hat{CH}_B(i) \;=\; \hat{CH}_B(i-1) \;\cap\; BAN(\theta_i) \tag{5.7}$$

Notice that the thresholding operation in (5.6) is simple enough to be implemented by means of a couple of base-limit registers. These registers should hold the values $C_{\min}(\theta)$ and $C_{\max}(\theta)$. However, the hardware look-up table has much more general scope, and it will be used in the following sections to compute other geometrical features. On the other hand, the intersection operation in (5.7) can be implemented by means of a simple pixel-by-pixel logical AND operation between the images $\hat{CH}_B(i-1)$ and $BAN(\theta_i)$.

Recapitulating, the complete algorithm for finding the approximated convex hull is as follows.

> *begin*
> $B :=$ input image;   /* digital blob */
> $A :=$ constant image;   /* $A(i,j) = 1$, for all i,j */
> /* A may be any approximation of the convex hull */
> *for* $i = 1$ *to* k *do begin*
>   generate ramp $C(\theta_i)$ and compute projection data;
>   find $C_{\min}(\theta_i)$ and $C_{\max}(\theta_i)$;
> $T :=$ threshold $C(\theta_i)$;   /* create band */
> $A := A$ AND T;
>   *end*;
> $\hat{CH}_B := A$;   /* approximated convex hull */
> *end*

It is obvious that the table look-up operations and the logical AND's can be performed in parallel hardware by handling multiple gray-level ramps in the same processor pass. This type of processing maps directly onto P^3E. Specifically, several arithmetic units generate coordinate-reference images for different orientations. These images are thresholded using look-up tables as that given in (5.6). These operations are performed in parallel at each ramp-generation/thresholding station. Each of these binary images is logically ANDed pixel-by-pixel with the current convex hull approximation obtained at the previous station. The new approximation is then fed to the next station.

Realistic applications may require the computation of $BAN(\theta)$ for many different θ's. Therefore, it seems reasonable to assume that at a certain step of the algorithm (due to the fixed number of ramp generators/ thresholding stations) a partial convex hull approximation will have to be temporarily stored in a binary image plane. After storing this partial result, we should continue the convex hull computation by using the same hardware resources for the remaining angles and the stored binary image as the present convex hull approximation.

We would like to remark that if only convex hulls are needed and some special hardware can be designed then a hardware histogrammer is not necessary for convex hull computations. It is clear that a much simpler hardware configuration can be used for the computation of C_{min} and C_{max} based on the coordinate-reference images. However, the above procedure is fully supported by P^3E. Each stage in the pipeline is devoted to generating a band at a certain orientation, and ANDing that band with the incoming convex hull image.

To illustrate the performance of the above algorithm, Fig. 5.1c shows an approximation of the convex hull for the blob given in Fig. 5.1a. These results were obtained by running the algorithm presented above in an IBM 7350 general purpose pipeline image processing system, where $k = 36$ different angles were used in the approximations.

Some remarks on the algorithm given above are in order. It is clear that the object B may not be digitally connected. In addition, the boundary of B may not be orientable (i.e., simple). Nevertheless, the procedure can be used to segment two objects whose convex hulls are disjoint, i.e., compute the approximate distance between their convex hulls and give the equations of separating semiplanes. The measurement of the approximate distance between the two convex hulls and the computation of separating semiplanes can be performed as follows. For each θ_i, the histogram of $C(\theta_i)$ masked by the binary image I can be used to detect whether the orientation θ_i corresponds to a semiplane which separates the convex hulls of two objects, O_1 and O_2. We find the smallest and largest zero entries, $C_1(\theta_i)$ and $C_2(\theta_i)$, within the interval of histogram entries $[C_{min}(\theta_i) + 1, C_{max}(\theta_i) - 1]$. These values may not exist, which would indicate that no digital semiplane with orientation θ_i can be found to separate O_1 from O_2; otherwise, all separating semiplanes in the direction θ_i are given by the equation:

$$\{(x,y): x\cos(\theta_i) + y\sin(\theta_i) \le b\} \tag{5.8}$$

where $b \in [C_1(\theta_i) - 1, C_2(\theta_i) + 1]$. The approximate distance between the two convex hulls is:[5]

$$\max_{1 \le i \le k} \{c_{\theta_i} \times [C_2(\theta_i) - C_1(\theta_i) + 2]\} \tag{5.9}$$

We would like to make a few comments about two additional features: diameter and enclosing box. It is clear that the diameter d can be readily approximated from the numbers $C_{\min}(\theta_i)$ and $C_{\max}(\theta_i)$ for $i = 1, \ldots, k$. The formula is

$$d \cong \max_{1 \le i \le k} \{c_{\theta_i} \times [C_{\max}(\theta_i) - C_{\min}(\theta_i)]\} \tag{5.10}$$

The difference $C_{\max}(\theta_i) - C_{\min}(\theta_i)$ is corrected by a factor c_{θ_i} which depends on the digital implementation of the coordinate-reference images.

Another important feature in applications is the enclosing box of an object. Notice that the enclosing box is nothing but a crude approximation of the convex hull. In other words, the box coordinates are given by $C_{\min}(0)$, $C_{\max}(0)$, $C_{\min}(90)$, and $C_{\max}(90)$. This feature could be implemented easily in a raster-logic architecture design, which is certainly *not* the case for the convex hull, diameter, and other related features.

Finally, we would like to remark that convex hull approximations, especially enclosing boxes, are usually needed in the form of digital images. This is important because these images carry important geometrical information which is used for further processing of the object, like the analysis of its concavities, etc., or ultimately for visual analysis of the results. Notice that if a sequence of coordinates constitute the output of an algorithm (as is the case in the classical random-access approach to the convex hull problem, enclosing box problem, etc.), the solution may be considered incomplete from the point of view of image analysis applications. In the classical algorithms one has to continue the process by *converting* between representations, i.e., to go from the sequence of coordinates (certainly not very useful for many applications of machine vision) to the image representation. Fortunately, this problem does not exist in

---

5 Note that $C_{\max}(\theta) - C_{\min}(\theta)$ may *not* measure the orthogonal distance between the parallel lines which are the borders of $BAN(\theta)$. See, for instance, (2.10).

our approach because of the efficient digital image representation of "bands" and its fast logical manipulation.

To end this section, we would like to point out that there are some other features which can be computed by using the pipeline approach. This is a direct consequence of the results presented in previous sections. It goes without saying that first order moments of a digital object can be readily computed from projection data obtained along parallel-line beams. Typical features such as centroid coordinates of a binary image can be obtained as a byproduct. For example, the mean value of the projection along C_0 is the x-coordinate of the centroid. Similarly, the y-coordinate is the mean of the projection along C_{90}. Higher order moments of these distributions can be also computed. More importantly, they can be obtained for *any* orientation θ yielding a rich description of the object.

In some applications, it is important to know high order "mixed" moments of an object. Let us take a simple example: covariance. This feature is important because is used in principal component analysis. Principal components analysis [Ande58] is a well known procedure for obtaining linear combinations of random or statistical variables for which the variance is maximized. It is a conventional way to obtain dimensionality reduction in pattern recognition applications [Prat78], and yields information concerning the orientation of the object. The principal components are the characteristic vectors of the covariance matrix of the distribution of pixels belonging to the object. The principal component corresponding to the largest characteristic root of the covariance matrix indicates the direction of the axis on which the projection of the object is the longest. The covariance matrix for objects in binary images is a 2×2 matrix. The diagonal elements of this matrix are the second order moments of the distribution of the x and y coordinates of pixels belonging to the object. The values of these moments can be found from the projections along C_0 and C_{90}. The off-diagonal elements are equivalent, and are equal to the covariance of the x and y coordinates of pixels belonging to the object. In order to compute the value of these elements, an image H is formed such that $H(x,y) = C_0(x,y) \times C_{90}(x,y)$, for all x and y (see Fig. 4.1d). The computation of this image can be accomplished more or less efficiently depending on the available general purpose image processing system. In some systems, the pixel-by-pixel product of two images can

50

be obtained in one processor pass. Consider the histogram of H counting only pixels belonging to the object. It is easy to show that the mean of this histogram is the expected value of the products of the x and y coordinates of pixels belonging to the object. This operation thus constitutes an interesting application of taking projections of binary objects along algebraic contours (in this case, the contours are hyperbolas). Therefore, the techniques given in Chap. 4 provide a fast method for computing the covariance of the object B. To complete the computation of the covariance, one should substract the product of the x and y coordinates of the centroid from the cross-moment obtained above. Once the covariance matrix is obtained, the computation of the characteristic roots and the characteristic vectors by the host computer is simple and fast.

An important remark concerning the features computed above is in order. If a digital image contains several digitally connected objects, then these algorithms can handle only one object at a time. Many applications would not suffer from this drawback. However, a reasonably reconfigurable pipeline system should allow the user to incorporate a dedicated "box" in which these features are computed for multi-object imagery. In this manner, features such as area, perimeter, centroids, etc., can be obtained for multi-object imagery in one-pass raster processing [Veil78, Vuyl81].

5.2 Computing Hough Transforms for Line and Curve Detection

One of the techniques for line or curve detection in digital images is the Hough transform [Duda72]. The transform is robust and is a good tool for boundary fitting in certain automated visual inspection applications [Dyer83]. In its original form, the Hough transform yields information concerning slopes and locations of lines in images. The Hough transform was generalized for detecting other non-linear patterns, adapted to use directional gradient information, and generalized to non-parametric curves [Ball82]. The reason for the robustness of the Hough transform and its variations [Duda72] is that these are global techniques. For example, in automated digital inspection applications, boundaries of manufactured objects are not perfect, and conventional digital edge detection techniques are sensitive to noise. Detected edges, which are expected to represent straight boundaries, are very often disconnected, fuzzy, and embedded in noise. The Hough transform is less sensitive to such discontinuities and noise since the decisions are made in the parameter space, where the information is global, and not locally in the image.

There are many practical applications in which fitting of straight boundaries to polygonal objects is a model driven operation. For such cases, the Hough transform can be drastically simplified due to the use of the apriori knowledge provided by the model. However, the well-known Hough transform and its offspring have all one common algorithmical feature: a large number of operations are applied to the coordinates of each pixel belonging to an object in order to compute the value of relevant parameters. The number of operations depends on the quantization of the parameter space and the number of parameters, as is the case for general parametrical curves. We will next show an alternate implementation which is well suited for real-time applications in general purpose pipeline image processing systems.

The Hough transform and some of its offspring are nothing but a maximum likelihood type detector applied over certain *projection data*. The maximum likelihood detection is applied because the position of the sought pattern in the parameter space is decided by choosing the most frequent value of the parameters. More importantly, the first step of Hough transform algorithms for detecting lines and other parametric curves is a particular case of projecting binary objects along general contours. Let us consider the case of detecting lines in digital images. The parameter space consists of all possible orientations and offsets for a line; in other words, if the line equation is given by $x \cos(\theta) + y \sin(\theta) = b$, the parameters are (θ, b). The technique then proceeds to update (i.e., increment by 1 or by a pixel dependent quantity) the corresponding parameters (θ, b) for each pixel in the binary image B. If the orientation parameter θ is quantized into a certain number of angles $\theta_1, \dots, \theta_k$, then for each θ_i, the projection of the binary image B along the family of digital parallel lines given by the ramp image C_{θ_i} corresponds to one slice of the Hough transform (i.e., for each discrete value k of the parameter b we count the number of pixels which belong to the digital straight line $\{ (x,y) : C_{\theta_i}(x,y) = k \}$). The comments given above readily extend to other patterns and parametrical curves such as ellipses, circles, hyperbolas, and so on.

Although this simple relationship between projection data and the Hough transform is rather evident, no one, as far we know, has used it in connection to architectures. The key aspect of this simple unification is that the results of Sects. 2.1,2 can be applied to the computation of the Hough transform. Therefore, as we will show next, the Hough transform technique can now be efficiently implemented in general purpose pipeline architectures.

In certain applications, we may know apriori the orientation of the lines to be fitted. Obviously this information is approximated, and therefore some tolerance $\delta\theta$ has to be used. Let us take a simple example. Figure 5.2a shows a binary image B. This is a typical gradient image of a printed circuit board. We need to fit lines to the boundaries of the conductor regions, which are known to have an orientation of 89°. Utilizing the technique describe in Chap. 2 we can compute the projections along $\theta = 89°$; in other words, one slice of the Hough transform. The result is given in Fig. 5.2b. As is clearly seen, the peaks of the histogram are the most likely position of the lines. As we remarked above, a more general situation will certainly involve the use of more angles. In this case, it is of the utmost importance to be able to generate multiple gray-levels images (ramps) and histograms in pipeline mode as in P^3E.

This algorithm has been implemented in several general purpose image processing pipelines (DeAnza and IBM 7350) and gives fast results when the search space is not too large. In any case, by pipelining a number of coordinate-reference generators and histogrammers in P^3E, we

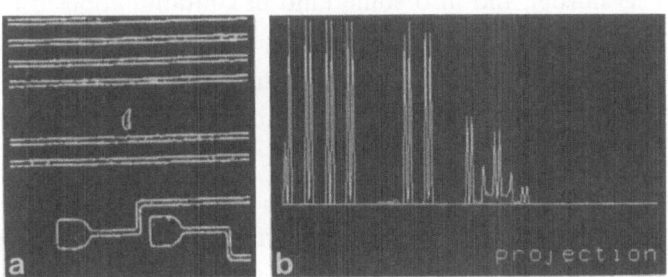

Fig. 5.2. (a) Gradient image of an industrial part, and (b) its projection along $\theta = 89°$

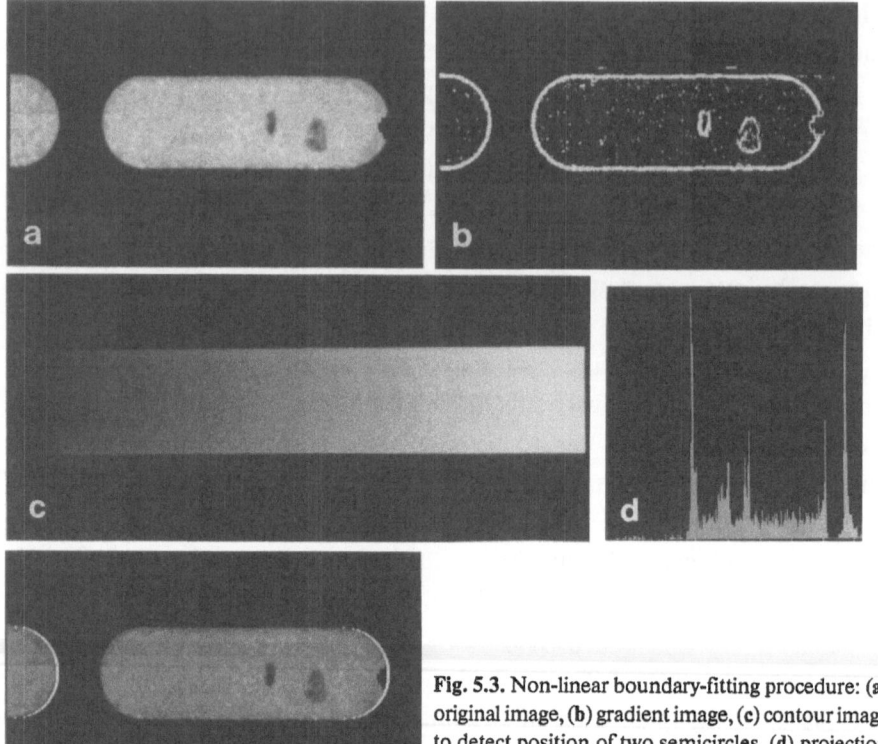

Fig. 5.3. Non-linear boundary-fitting procedure: (a) original image, (b) gradient image, (c) contour image to detect position of two semicircles, (d) projection along contour image, and (e) detected semicircles overlaid on original image

will get a very fast implementation of the Hough transform in this kind of general purpose architecture (see Chap. 3).

To end this section, we would like to give an interesting example about the use of projection data for curved contours. Let us take the image of an industrial part given in Fig. 5.3a. This part has defects (for example, a chip in its border and also some kind of contamination in its interior). We follow a global approach to analyze the boundaries of the part, knowing apriori that the curved section of the boundary is a semicircle. We first fit the straight lines of the boundary, by applying the above pipeline implementation for line fitting to the gradient image shown in Fig. 5.3b. Once these two lines are fitted we proceed to detect the curved parts of the boundary. We need to generated a ramp image as that in Fig. 5.3c. This image is obtained by using the formula $R_X + \sqrt{r^2 - (R_Y - y_c)^2}$ where r and y_c are the radius and y-coordinate of the circles to fit (these parameters are immediately obtained from the position of the lines fitted before). Also, if the square root is undefined, the result of the complete operation is, say, zero. It is interesting to note that this operation is performed easily by using the same resources as those described in Fig. 3.1. The operation $\sqrt{r^2 - (R_Y - y_c)^2}$ is performed by applying table look-up to the image register R_Y. The function of the CIG is just to add this value to the register R_X. The projection of the gradient image along this coordinate-reference ramp is shown in Fig. 5.3d. It is seen that the position of the two highest peaks indicate the most likely values of the center of the sought circles. The positions of the detected circles in the pattern of Fig. 5.3d are shown in Fig. 5.3e (overlaid on the original image). An analogous approach is followed for detecting the other semicircle in the boundary.

As we remarked above, the update of Hough parameters can be made with a pixel-dependent quantity (not necessarily 0 or 1). In the modified Hough transform, the increment is the value of a gradient of the original image. This transform can also be supported by P^3E since it becomes the projection of the gradient image. As an example, Fig. 5.4a shows a gradient of an image, and Figs. 5.4b,c depict its projection along $\theta = 0°$ and $\theta = 51°$, respectively.

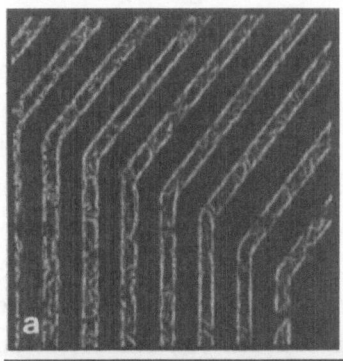

Fig. 5.4. (a) Gray-level gradient image, and its projections along 0° (b) and 51° (c) (modified Hough transform)

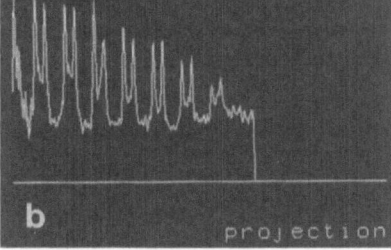

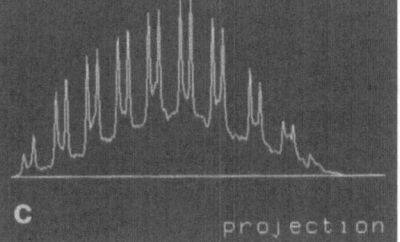

5.3 Generating Polygonal Masks

Applications in computer graphics where one needs to "color" or "fill" regions are well known in the scientific community [Pavl78b]. On the contrary, the use of *mask images* in machine vision or image analysis applications may not be so popular as in computer graphics. The simplest case of a digital mask is a binary image M which takes the values 0 or 1 for all its pixels. An example of the use of such a mask is for selective application of an operator on a gray-level picture I. Specifically, if O denotes a digital operator (such as convolution, histogramming, etc.) only the pixels of I signaled in M are taken into consideration by O. For example, in a histogramming operation, only those pixels in $I(i,j)$ such that $M(i,j) = 1$ are histogrammed, and those for which $M(i,j) = 0$ are ignored.

In machine vision applications, the mask conveys some information which for processing purposes may be needed in the form of a digital picture. This information may relate to a variety of sources. In the histogramming example given above, the mask M may represent points of high gradient in I, which is significant for image interpretation purposes. In particular, histogramming those pixels in I whose gradient is "high" yields some useful thresholding techniques for image segmentation [Wezs78].

A natural question can now be raised: why should this information be represented in the form of a digital mask image? The reason for this question may well be that the mask M is, in the worst case, a set of random pixels which can ultimately be represented as a sequence of pixel coordinates. In addition, if the set of coordinates has some special geometrical arrangement (as in a polygonal shape) a more compact representation can be used, such as the equations of the boundary of the polygon. The answer to the above question is that the convenience of an image representation for M is dictated by the architecture where the operator O is implemented. As will be seen below, conveying geometrical information in the form of digital images may be a *must* for implementation purposes in pipelines.

As suggested above, there may be certain cases where the information to be conveyed in the mask is *geometrical*. For example, the mask image

M can be a digital approximation of a polygon, or more generally, a set of polygons in which each polygon is assigned a different color or code. In this case, the mask M is no longer a binary image. Pipeline image processors do not allow for efficient random access to the image memory planes. Random access is accomplished through Direct Memory Access (DMA) by the supporting host micro-computer. Therefore, algorithms utilizing DMA heavily tend to be fairly slow since the processing power of the pipeline is not used.

There is another limitation in some commercially available systems which is the impossibility of accessing image-plane pixel coordinates during a processor pass. This feature may suggest that algorithms involving manipulation of pixel coordinates are either impossible or too slow to be run in pipeline systems. However, we have shown above that fast algorithms can be obtained for Hough transforms, projections of images (such as the Radon transform), convex hulls, and other geometrical features, even though they require pixel coordinate manipulation (see also [Sanz87b]). Classical implementations of these algorithms require random access and pixel coordinate handling. In these pipeline processors, some digital operators can be selectively applied by indicating to the processor the pixels to be taken into consideration. Except for rectangular boundaries which can be handled by four registers, there is no other way one can communicate *geometrical* information to the processor but in the form of digital mask images. For example, if the histogram of a gray-level image I is desired just for pixels belonging to a certain polygonal area, this polygon must be given in the form of a mask image M. In this way, the processor can compute the histogram of I only for those pixels such that $M(i,j) = 1$. It may appear at first glance that the need for a mask representation constitutes a disadvantage of pipelines because representing one or more regions in a digital image with different codes is a time consuming task. However, it was shown that such is not the case [Sanz87a].

It is important to remark that other image-oriented architectures can be used for polygonal mask computations. Cellular array computers are a reasonable alternative since each processor can be devoted to verifying logical propositions describing the polygons. Particularly appealing are the MIMD/SIMD models presented in [Rice85]. More complex M/SIMD machines [Ibra85] or even systolic networks [Hara85] should also be explored.

Several classical approaches known in computer graphics can be used for generating mask images [Crow77, Dist82, Lieb78, Newm79]. For a single-polygon mask, these procedures have two common features:

1. First, the boundary of the polygon must be drawn on the image plane. In certain cases[Ackl81], this must be done by conveying boundary information in the form of pixel flags.

2. After the previous step is completed, the polygon interior must be filled in from its boundary. This is accomplished by knowing the coordinate of least one interior pixel or by raster-scan processing.

Although certain extensions of the existing procedures were recently obtained for multi-polygon images, there are some limitations in implementing any of these techniques in pipeline processors. The reason is that these approaches require random access of the image planes, manipulation of pixel coordinates, and specialized raster logic.

It is necessary to clarify that "binary digital polygonal mask" should be understood to mean a (0-1) image where the set of pixels with value 1 describe a digital approximation of a polygon. In other words, if P denotes such a polygon, [6] we would like to obtain an image I_s such that

$$I_s(i,j) = \begin{cases} 1 & \text{if } (i,j) \in P \\ 0 & \text{otherwise} \end{cases} \tag{5.11}$$

More generally, we may be given more than one polygon simultaneously. In this case, we would like to assign different codes to each polygon in the image. In other words, if $Q_1, Q_2, \ldots, Q_n$ are the given polygons (whose interiors are assumed disjoint), we wish to obtain an image I_m such that for all $k = 1, \ldots, n,$

---

6 The transition between continuous and discrete geometries will not be discussed here. It is enough to assume that P is obtained from a continuous polygon P_c by a certain discretization process or mapping. For example, the interior (boundary) pixels of P refer to those pixels in the discrete plane which come via the mapping from points in the topological interior (boundary) of P_c. We will show some discretization mappings which are suitable for efficient pipeline processor computation.

$$I_m(i,j) = \begin{cases} c_k, & \text{if } (i,j) \in \dot{Q}_k \\ d_{l_1...l_s}, & \text{if } (i,j) \in \overset{s}{\underset{h=1}{\cap}} \gamma Q_{l_h} \\ b & \text{(background color),} \quad \text{otherwise} \end{cases}$$ (5.12)

where b and the c's and d's are different codes, and $\dot{Q}_k$, γQ_k denote the interior and the boundary of the polygon Q_k. Note that (5.12) differentiates between the following three situations:

i) a pixel (i,j) belongs to a single polygon

ii) a pixel (i,j) belongs to the boundary of one or more polygons

iii) a pixel (i,j) does not belong to any of the given polygons (i.e., it is a background pixel)

A simple example showing the multi-coloring process is given in Fig. 5.5. In this image, three polygons P_1, P_2, and P_3 are drawn, and their interiors receive colors c_1, c_2, and c_3, respectively. Note that only two polygons are convex: P_2 and P_3. The boundary between P_1 and the background receives the color d_1. Similarly, d_3 is the color assigned to the boundary

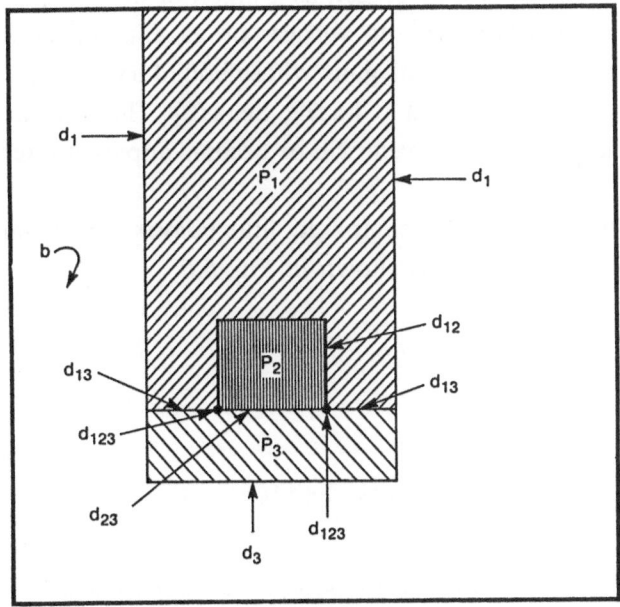

Fig. 5.5. Multi-coloring of a set of polygons

59

of P_3 and the background. In addition, d_{12}, d_{13}, and d_{23} are codes given to the common boundary between P_1 and P_2, P_1 and P_3, P_2 and P_3, respectively. Finally, the *two* points resulting from the intersection of the boundaries of the three polygons are labeled d_{123} while pixels not belonging to any polygon are labeled with b (background color).

A straightforward approach to the multi-coloring problem is to treat each polygon Q_k separately. In other words, a certain procedure can be applied as many times as the number of given polygons. Each time a polygon is colored, a different code is assigned and the images so obtained are then combined into a single image. On the other hand, the approach presented in this section will produce the coloring by treating all the polygons at once.

The polygonal mask image generation process requires an appropriate description of the polygons $P, Q_1, \ldots, Q_n$. This description (or representation) consists of finding certain properties and computing geometrical features of the polygons. The optimal solution to this problem and the kind of information needed depend on the approach followed to solve the mask generation problem. For example, one may wish to compute the vertices of each polygon (from the equations of its boundary lines) and order them in a clockwise mode (if the polygon is non-self-intersecting). Another possibility is to represent the polygon as a union of the triangles arising from Delaunay's tesselation of its vertices or as a union of a minimum possible number of convex polygons whose boundary lines are given by those of the original polygon [Chaz79, Scha78]. The specific meaning of *polygon model* for our approach will be become apparent later in this section.

Suppose that a polygon P is decomposed into convex polygonal components having disjoint interiors as shown in Fig. 5.6.

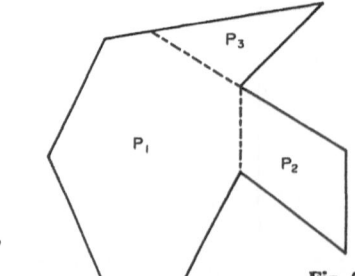

Fig. 5.6. Partition of a polygon into convex components

In other words, the polygon is represented as a union of convex polygons $P_1, P_2, \ldots, P_m$ whose boundary lines are known.

$$P = \bigcup_{i=1}^{m} P_i \qquad (5.13)$$

P^3E (along with other general purpose image processing systems) has the hardware capability to take logical OR operations on a pixel-by-pixel basis over two or more digital images. Therefore, our problem becomes to efficiently compute the mask-image representation I_s (5.11) for a convex polygon. After doing this for all the convex components P_i, a final OR (which usually takes an extra pass through the image processor) of all the convex polygonal masks will solve the problem.

A convex polygon is the intersection of a finite number of semi-planes, i.e.,

$$P = \bigcap_{i=1}^{s} A_i \qquad (5.14)$$

where

$$A_i = \{(x,y): x\cos(\theta_i) + y\sin(\theta_i) \leq n_i\} \qquad (5.15)$$

The key issue is how to obtain in a highly efficient way the mask-image representation I_s (5.11) of a semi-plane. After this is done, a multiple (pixel-by-pixel) AND operation among all the images defining the semi-planes A_i's will compute the sought image. Finding the image representation of a given semi-plane in P^3E and other general purpose image processing architectures is the goal of the discussion that follows.

A digital semi-plane image whose boundary line has slope $\tan(\theta)$, for $0 \leq \theta < 180$ may be considered as a thresholded image of a digital ramp of gray values. This thresholding operation is a simple task in general purpose image processing architectures. It can be accomplished by passing the image C_0 through a look-up table T predefined with one of the following two functions:

$$T_1(g) = \begin{cases} 1 & \text{if } g \leq n \\ 0 & \text{otherwise} \end{cases} \qquad (5.16)$$

or

$$T_2(g) = \begin{cases} 1 & \text{if } g \geq n \\ 0 & \text{otherwise} \end{cases} \qquad (5.17)$$

The semi-plane image is now obtained as $T_1(C_\theta(i,j))$ or $T_2(C_\theta(i,j))$, for all pixels (i,j). The information on whether a certain pixel of the ramp C_θ should be mapped into a "0" or a "1" is obtained from the model of the polygon (therefore, it is known which of the look-up tables (5.16) or (5.17) should be used). Figure 5.7 shows a mask representation of a certain horizontal semi-plane by using the ramp C_{150}.

Fig. 5.7. Binary representation of a semiplane

Notice that a similar thresholding operation to that of (5.16,17) can be used to obtain a mask-image representation of a "band" $B_\theta^{n_1 n_2}$. This band may be useful if this boundary configuration is recognized in the model of the polygon. In other words, the ramp C_θ can be used at the thresholding operation to obtain a binary-image mask of a "band" B, as follows:

$$B_\theta^{n_1 n_2}(i,j) = \begin{cases} 1 & \text{if } n_1 \leq C_\theta(i,j) \leq n_2 \\ 0 & \text{otherwise} \end{cases} \qquad (5.18)$$

In some commercially available systems, the algorithm presented in this section for the binary polygonal mask generation takes $\sum_{i=1}^{m} (2K_i + 1)$ processor passes, where K_i is the number of boundary lines of the ith polygonal component of P. The estimated number of passes given above is certainly the worst-case complexity. The possibility of generating "bands" instead of semi-planes as described in (5.18) can be used to speed up the polygonal mask generation for special polygonal shapes. As an example, let us take the very simple case of the polygon given in Fig. 5.8. In this particular situation, we will need only two ramps, only one extra pass per convex polygon (P_1 and P_2 in the figure), plus a final OR of the two images so obtained. This requires only seven passes for the IBM

 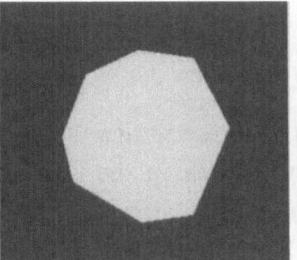 

Fig. 5.8. Special binary polygon **Fig. 5.9.** Convex polygon   **Fig. 5.10.** Complex polygon

7350 architecture. In addition, Fig. 5.9 shows another polygon, in this case convex, generated by using gray-level ramps at different angles. On the other hand, Fig. 5.10 shows the mask obtained for a more complicated polygonal pattern. In conventional general purpose image processing systems where a processor pass for 512 × 512 images is performed at TV rates, the algorithms presented here take a small fraction of a second for simple polygonal shapes.

We would like to remark that in many image analysis problems the mask generation process is not an isolated operation. The mask creation arises usually from the need of framing objects or their component regions. For example, the Hough transform technique to fit lines to the boundaries of digital polygonal objects in image analysis pipeline architectures, presented in Sect. 5.2, requires the computation of a gray-level ramp for each direction of the boundary lines of the polygon. In P^3E, many coordinate-reference generators are linked together. In this way, many line orientations can be handled in a single processor pass. P^3E thus offers a large degree of parallelism in the computation of binary masks [Sanz87a].

5.4 Generating Multi-Colored Masks

In this section, a generalization of the technique proposed in Sect. 5.3 is presented. This algorithm can be used to generate multi-tone polygonal masks and, in particular, binary polygonal masks. In fact, if the algorithm of this section is used for binary masks, an extremely appealing alternative to the technique given in Sect. 5.3 will be obtained.

63

Assume that $L_1, ..., L_r$ are the boundary lines of the given polygons $Q_1, ..., Q_n$. We will generate a tesselation of the image plane into convex polygons of dimension two or less. We will then show a procedure to obtain a digital image with this tesselation in which each convex component is assigned a different code. Each of the lines L_k determines two disjoint open semi-planes, $S^+(L_k)$ and $S^-(L_k)$. If $P_1, ..., P_s$ are convex polygons of a tesselation with r lines (for $r = 1$, $P_1 = S^+(L_1)$, $P_2 = S^-(L_1)$, and $P_3 = L_1$) and L_{r+1} is a new line, then the elements of the new tesselation are:

$$S^+(L_{r+1}) \cap P_1, ..., S^+(L_{r+1}) \cap P_s,$$

$$S^-(L_{r+1}) \cap P_1, ..., S^-(L_{r+1}) \cap P_s,$$

$$L_{r+1} \cap P_1, ..., L_{r+1} \cap P_s$$

It is trivial to prove that the polygons which form the tesselation are convex, disjoint and cover the whole 2-D plane. A more practical and less cumbersome way of visualizing the tesselation generated by $L_1, ..., L_r$ is as follows. Draw all lines $L_1, ..., L_r$; the resulting segments (with no end-points), vertices (end-points), and convex regions (not containing segments or vertices but having them as boundaries) form the tesselation. As a simple example, Fig. 5.11 shows the tesselation obtained by using the lines which are boundaries of the polygons shown in Fig. 5.5.

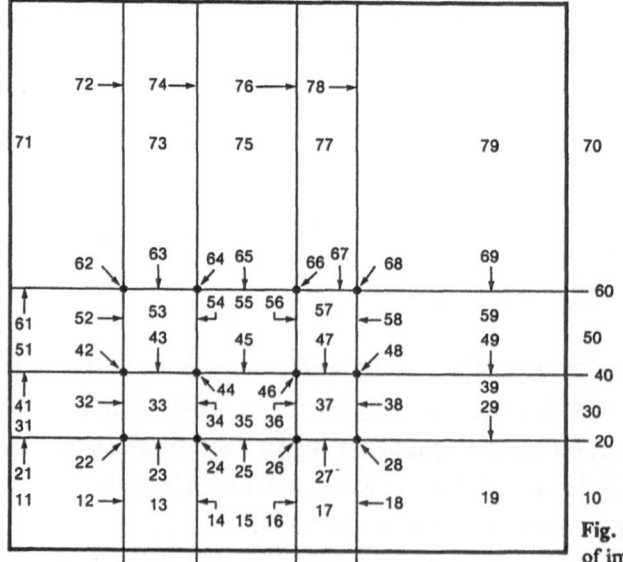

Fig. 5.11. Geometrical tesselation of image

64

We will now discuss how this tesselation can be efficiently generated in image processing pipeline architectures in a way that each component receives a distinct code. Let us assign different codes to the semi-planes $S^+(L_k)$ and $S^-(L_k)$, and to the line L_k as well. By assigning codes we really mean generating an image where these three zones receive different codes. To accomplish this operation, we refer back to the discussion of the binary mask generation algorithm. All we need to do is create a ramp image with the orientation of line L_k and pass this ramp through a look-up table. This look-up table is slightly more complicated than those in (5.16,17):

$$T'(g) = \begin{cases} t_{k_1}, & \text{if } g > n_k \\ t_{k_2}, & \text{if } g = n_k \\ t_{k_3}, & \text{if } g < n_k \end{cases} \qquad (5.19)$$

where n_k is such that $L_k = \{(x,y):x\cos(\theta) + y\sin(\theta) = n_k\}$, and the t's are codes.

After this operation is performed for each component line L_k, we combine all the images so obtained by some logical or arithmetic operation. There are several alternatives, and the optimal choice depends on many factors: number of lines, available resources in the supporting architecture, etc. The goal of this combination of images is to obtain a tesselation of the image plane in which each convex component (for all possible dimensions, i.e., 2 for regions with non-empty interior, 1 for segments, and 0 for vertices) receives a different code. In order that the regions of this tesselation have distinct codes which identify them uniquely, we must assign suitable numbers to the partial codes $t_{k_1}, t_{k_2}, t_{k_3}$ (see (5.19)). A possible solution is to assign different prime numbers to the partial codes $t_{k_1}, t_{k_2}, t_{k_3}$ for all k's, and then combine the images obtained by the table look-up given by (5.19) into a multiple pixel-by-pixel product. Taking products may not be desirable, since the resulting codes may become excessively large even for a small number of lines.

An alternative is to perform a pixel-by-pixel addition over all the images. In this case the partial codes (see (5.19)) should be assigned in a way such that the resulting *sum* of the images define the desired regions of the tesselation uniquely. It is simple to devise such a technique. One possibility is as follows. Suppose that the polygons $Q_1, Q_2, ..., Q_n$ are such that there are M_k lines at the same angle θ_k, where $k = 1, \ldots, K$, and K is the number of different orientations. Denote by $L_{km}, m = 1, \ldots, M_k$ the lines at orientation θ_k and respective offsets $N_{k1} < N_{k2} < \ldots < N_{kM_k}$. We now define a set of look-up tables $T_1, \ldots, T_k$ to accomplish the image tesselation by exploiting the fact that only one ramp is necessary per line orientation. The look-up table associated with the direction θ_k should be defined as follows (let $N_{k0} = 0$)

$$
T_k(g) = \begin{cases}
t_k, & \text{if } g = 0 \\
(2m - 1)t_k, & \text{if } N_{k(m-1)} < g < N_{km} \\
2mt_k, & \text{if } g = N_{km} \\
(2M_k + 1)t_k, & \text{if } N_{kM_k} < g
\end{cases}
\tag{5.20}
$$

where $m = 1, 2, \ldots, M_k$, and the colors are given by $t_k = (2M_{k-1} + 1)t_{k-1} + 1, t_1 = 1$.

Each ramp is passed through the corresponding look-up table and the thresholded images are fed to an ALU for pixel-by-pixel summation. The image T so obtained has the property that any two pixels in T are assigned the same code if and only if they belong to the same component of the tesselation. The proof of this property is shown in [Sanz87a]. Figure 5.11 shows a family of lines and the corresponding tesselation obtained by applying the above strategy. The codes assigned to each line are shown outside the square frame indicating the border of the digital image.

We should remark that the only information about the given polygons $Q_1, \ldots, Q_n$ which has been used so far is the equations of their boundary lines. The next step is to integrate different fragments of the polygons Q_k given by the convex components of the tesselation. Since we assume that the necessary information about the reconstruction of Q_k's is available from the model, the union of the different fragments of each Q_k can be accomplished very efficiently by means of a table look-up operation. Recall that the code $\bar{c}_k$ of each component of the tesselation is unique. Therefore, the look-up table should be loaded in such a way that the codes which correspond to a certain region of interest are mapped into the same number. This number will thereon identify the region (we denote the numbers of the regions by $r_1, r_2, \ldots$). A sample scheme of this operation implemented by a look-up table $RLUT$ is as follows.

Tesselation component codes	Final region of interest codes
$\bar{c}_1$	r_1
$\bar{c}_2$	r_1
$\bar{c}_3$	r_2
$\bar{c}_4$	r_3
$\bar{c}_5$	r_2
$\bar{c}_6$	r_1
.	.
.	.
.	.

At this point, different "semantics" (i.e., region models) can be used to join several convex components of the tesselation into single regions. This information about the problem has to be provided apriori in the form of what we have called the *model*. Constructing the model is an "off-line" operation and should be performed just once. The derivation of the final look-up table, i.e., figuring out which codes arise in the tesselation and which polygons they belong to, can be done either manually (for simple cases) or by means of an interactive computer graphics program.

The complete algorithm presented in this section is as follows.

```
begin
Tess(i,j) = 0,  for all (i,j);
for  k = 1 to K  do begin
          R := generate_ramp (θₖ) ;
          Tess(i,j) = Tess(i,j) + Tₖ(R(i,j)), for all (i,j);
          end;
CM(i,j) = RLUT(Tess(i,j)),  for all (i,j);
end
```

The digital tesselation shown in Fig. 5.12 was generated using the present algorithm in a Deanza image processor and the model was prepared manually. Figure 5.13a shows the table used to reconstruct the polygon shown in white in Fig. 5.13b, based on the lines and tesselation given in Fig. 5.12. Note that this multi-coloring algorithm can be used for generating binary masks, thus providing an appealing alternative to the technique presented in Sect. 5.3.

Fig. 5.12. Digital tesselation of image

Code of Tessellation Component		Code of Region
44 (point)	$\longrightarrow$	r_2
45 (segment)	$\longrightarrow$	r_2
46 (point)	$\longrightarrow$	r_2
56 (segment)	$\longrightarrow$	r_2
66 (point)	$\longrightarrow$	r_2
65 (segment)	$\longrightarrow$	r_2
64 (point)	$\longrightarrow$	r_2
54 (segment)	$\longrightarrow$	r_2
55 (open polygon)	$\longrightarrow$	r_2

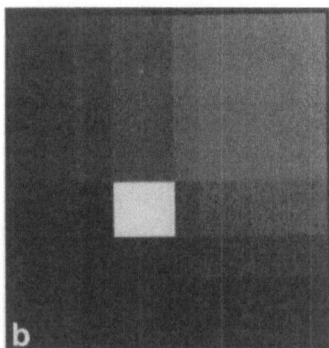

Fig. 5.13. (a) Look-up table for reconstructing polygon P_2 from components of tesselation, and (b) reconstruction of polygon P_2 from components of tesselation

We should emphasize that P^3E can drastically improve the speed of the algorithm presented, since multiple ramp images can be generated and thresholded during one processor pass. In a subsequent pass, these thresholded images are then combined via pixel-by-pixel logical operations in the ALU at each stage, with the resulting multi-color mask appearing at the output.

5.5 Non-Linear Masks

The algorithms given in Sects. 5.3,4 can be extended to other masks where the shape is not necessarily polygonal. In fact, the pixel coordinate manipulation concepts and P^3E can be used for generating second order polynomial ramps or other more complex patterns. The ideas are completely analogous since similar digital tesselations to those of Sect. 5.4 can be generated by using non-linear boundaries. To this end, the CIG's should be powerful enough to compute non-linear coordinate references. As an example, let us return for a moment to the example of Fig. 5.3 given in Sect. 5.2. It is seen that to complete the analysis of defects in the boundaries of the part further work is necessary. For example, we may have to measure how much the defect in the boundary deviates from a good part. In order to do this, it seems very convenient to generate the mask of what would be the ideal part (where the parameters are given by those of the present piece). To this end, we can generate a binary mask by thresholding the contour image of Fig. 5.3d. This non-linear mask is shown in Fig. 5.14.

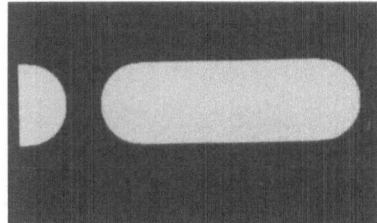

Fig. 5.14. Non-linear binary mask

Lastly, if a few more powerful features are added to the CIG in Fig. 3.1, more general patterns can be obtained. It is particularly appealing to be able to take the maximum and minimum between two or more images in a pixel-by-pixel mode. For example, if the CIG can compute the maximum (or the minimum) between the pixel generated at the CIG and the current pixel entering the stage, more complicated patterns can be generated. One possibility is shown in Fig. 5.15. By using these patterns and applying multi-level thresholds as before, we can get more sophisticated shapes. For example, Fig. 5.16 shows the image obtained

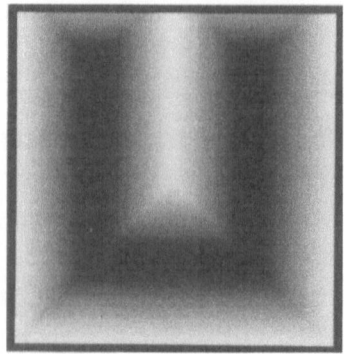 

Fig. 5.15. Contour ramp obtained by using pixel-by-pixel maxima and minima

Fig. 5.16. Shape obtained by thresholding a contour image

from a contour image generated by taking maxima and minima among circular, elliptical, and linear ramps. The way to control the formation of these images and to relate them to user-specified shapes are some subjects of our current research interest.

6. P³E-Based Image Processing Algorithms and Techniques

The impetus for this chapter lies in determining the *completeness* of our model, i.e., determining whether or not the same architecture is appropriate for obtaining a digital approximation not only to the Radon transform, but also to the *inverse* Radon transform. Thus, we have focussed on image processing applications in which Radon data must be backprojected to recover the image. These applications are presented in the following sections, and they include: (1) digital image reconstruction using the non-iterative techniques of convolution backprojection and filtered backprojection; (2) digital image reconstruction using the iterative Kacmarz method; (3) 2-D convolution of an image with a kernel; (4) rotation and translation of images; and (5) CT reconstruction, which uses exact sampled-continuous as opposed to digital projection data. In all of the experiments, we used 256 × 256 8-bit images. We utilized 180 projections for each image, at orientations $\theta = 0°, 1°, 2°, \dots, 179°$. As will be seen, our model *is* complete, and the architecture presented in Chap. 3 *does* support both the projection and backprojection operations.

6.1 Non-iterative Reconstruction

For non-iterative image reconstruction, we start with the conventional definition for the inverse Radon transform [Helg80], i.e.:

$$f(x,y) = \int_0^\pi Q_\theta(t)d\theta \tag{6.1}$$

where $Q_\theta(t)$ is the projection $P_\theta(t)$ filtered by a 1-D filter whose frequency response is $|\xi|$ (ξ denotes spatial frequency). A discrete approximation to this integral is of the form:

$$f(j\delta, i\delta) \cong \frac{\pi}{M} \sum_{n=1}^{M} Q_{\theta n}(j\cos\theta_n + i\sin\theta_n) \qquad (6.2)$$

where the projections $P_\theta(t)$ are known for the M angles θ_n. This operation is extremely simple. Paraphrased, it states that once the filtered projections are obtained, an image pixel is reconstructed by summing over all orientations the contribution from each filtered projection. This contribution for a given orientation is simply the value from the filtered projection corresponding to the contour that contains the image pixel. Thus, assuming that the pixel falls on the kth contour at orientation θ_i, the contribution from θ_i is simply $Q_{\theta i}(k)$!

Reconstructing an image in this way is clearly a non-iterative procedure, and depending upon the filtering method used it is referred to as the *filtered backprojection* or *convolution backprojection* technique. Of course, filtering the projections is a separate problem from distributing the filtered projections back over the image. Filtering the projections is essentially a signal processing issue, and we will return to it later. The process of reconstruction once the projections are filtered, however, is paramount to the completeness and applicability of our model.

We call the operation of distributing the filtered projection values back over the image *backtracing*. As we will show, this operation fits nicely into the framework of our model. To illustrate, once the projections have been filtered, we proceed as follows. First, we start with a null image. At a given orientation, for each pixel in the image, we compute the corresponding contour value, use it to address a value in the filtered projection array (i.e., through a LUT operation), and add that value to the image pixel. This procedure is performed for all orientations to obtain the reconstructed image unscaled by the factor π/M. This scaling may either be performed on the filtered projections before backtracing, or on the image afterward.

This algorithm, in the context of our model, conforms easily to a pipelined implementation. The generation of contour pixel values may be pipelined with the access of projection array values and the subsequent backtracing summation. The backtracing operation at one orientation can be pipelined with that at the next, since only one pixel is operated on at a time. Finally, the reconstructed image may be generated in raster mode, since each pixel is visited only once at each orientation.

72

The entire procedure is fully supported by the architecture presented in Chap. 3. Recall that we included additional hardware to satisfy the requirements of the above reconstruction algorithm. First, since the algorithm requires that each of the projections be filtered, we included 1-D signal processing capability in the form of a chip for each pipeline stage. Thus, the need for host processing of the projection data is eliminated. Also, recall that we included an ALU in each stage for performing simple operations on the incoming image pixels. In the above algorithm, this ALU is necessary for adding the backtraced value to the incoming image pixel, before passing the accumulated result on to the next stage.

We now turn to the problem of filtering the projections. The filter function $|\xi|$ required by the inverse Radon transform emphasizes high spatial frequencies. We can expect any projection data collected using our model to have low signal-to-noise ratios at high frequencies, due to the nature of the digital approximations we make. Needless to say, use of the above filter will result in noise amplification. Several non-optimal bandlimiting window functions have been proposed to limit the unbounded nature of the frequency response. These include, in order of increasing high frequency suppression: the Ram-Lak filter, the Shepp-Logan filter, the lowpass cosine window, and the generalized lowpass Hamming window. The frequency responses of these filters are given in Table 6.1. Note that by using these filters, one is exchanging image resolution for noise suppression. In our experiments, we have found that the lowpass cosine filter generally produces the most visually pleasing reconstructions, and, unless otherwise stated, it is used for all the reconstruction results shown here.

If convolution in projection space is used to perform the filtering, the above reconstruction algorithm is referred to as the *convolution backprojection* technique. If the filtering is performed in Fourier space, however, the algorithm is designated the *filtered backprojection* technique. As expected, both techniques produce comparable results. We have implemented both in our experiments, and have found that the results are virtually indistinguishable (given an adequate number of samples in the discrete impulse response for convolution, an adequate number of elements in the DFT sequences, an adequate amount of zero-padding in the DFT data, etc.). For comparison, in Sects. 6.1.1 and 6.1.2 we show

Table 6.1. Non-optimal bandlimiting window functions

Filter	Frequency Response
Ram-Lak	$H_{rl}(\xi) = \mid \xi \mid \Pi(\xi d)$
Shepp-Logan	$H_{sl}(\xi) = \mid \xi \mid sinc(\xi d)\Pi(\xi d)$
Lowpass Cosine Window	$W_{lc}(\xi) = \cos(\pi \xi d)\Pi(\xi d)$
Generalized Lowpass Hamming Window	$W_{glh}(\xi) = [\alpha + (1 - \alpha)\cos(2\pi\xi d)]\Pi(\xi d),$ $0 \le \alpha \le 1$

Notes and Notation:

(1) $d \equiv \dfrac{1}{2\xi_0}$, where ξ_0 is the highest spatial frequency of interest in the image.

(2) $\Pi(\xi d)$ is the rectangle function, defined as:

$$\Pi(\xi d) = \begin{cases} 1 & \mid \xi d \mid < \dfrac{1}{2} \\ 0 & \mid \xi d \mid > \dfrac{1}{2} \end{cases}$$

(3) The lowpass cosine and generalized lowpass Hamming windows formally belong to the class of filters:

$$H(\xi) = \mid \xi \mid W(\xi)$$

where $W(\xi)$ is a bandlimiting window function. This class of filters is a generalization of the Ram-Lak filter.

reconstructions of the same image using both techniques. However, for brevity in later applications, we will refrain from presenting duplicate results using both techniques. Instead, we will rely solely on the filtered backprojection technique.

6.1.1 Convolution Backprojection

For the convolution backprojection technique, then, the reconstruction algorithm consists of the following two steps:

1. Convolve the projections with the discrete impulse response of the filter to obtain the filtered projections.
2. Backtrace the filtered projections.

An image of an English village is shown in Fig. 6.1a. A horizontal profile of this image is displayed in Fig. 6.1b. The projection space

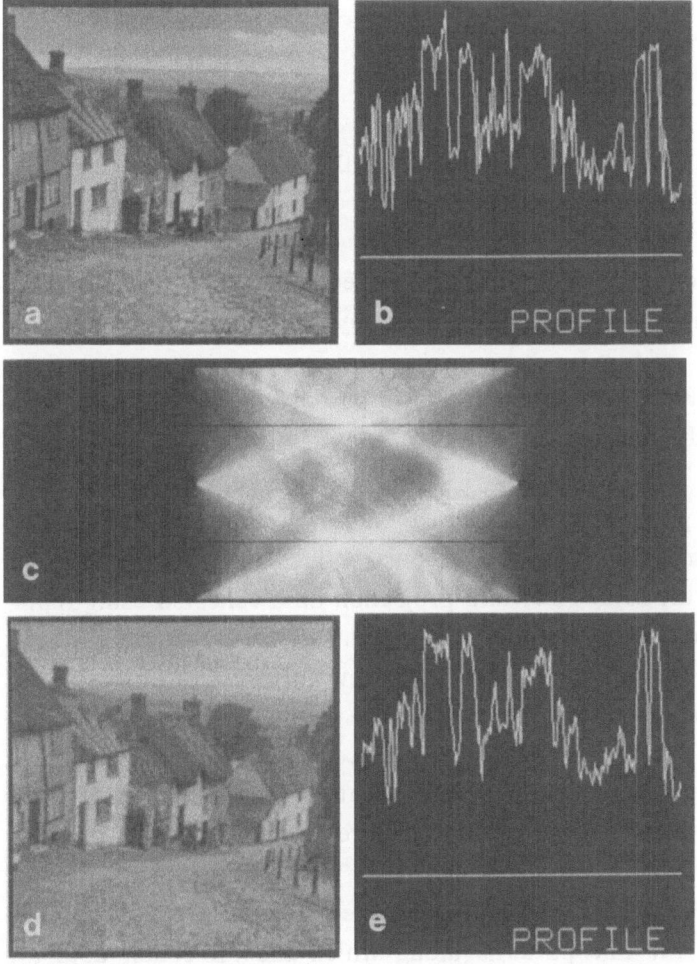

Fig. 6.1. (a) Village image, (b) horizontal profile, (c) projection space representation, (d) reconstruction via convolution backprojection, and (e) horizontal profile of reconstruction

representation of this image is shown in Fig. 6.1c, with θ varying from $0°$ to $179°$ along the vertical axis. The projections are all centered about $t = 0$. The top and bottom dark horizontal lines correspond to $\theta = 45°$ and $135°$, respectively. This data was collected using representation I for the contours. Using the lowpass cosine filter and the above projection data, the convolution backprojection technique yields the reconstruction shown in part d of Fig. 6.1. The corresponding profile is shown in part e. As is seen, the noise in the projection data has resulted in a noisy reconstruction. The quality of the reconstruction can be greatly improved by using projection data collected using representation II for the contours, as will be shown using the filtered backprojection technique.

6.1.2 Filtered Backprojection

For the filtered backprojection technique, the reconstruction algorithm consists of the following four steps:

1. Take the Fourier transform of the projections.
2. Multiply the transformed projections by the frequency response of the filter.
3. Take the inverse Fourier transform to obtain the filtered projections.
4. Backtrace the filtered projections.

As stated previously, the filtered backprojection and convolution backprojection techniques produce reconstructions of similar quality. To illustrate, using the same filter and projection data collected using representation I, the reconstruction obtained for the village image using filtered backprojection is shown in Fig. 6.2a. The new horizontal profile is shown in Fig. 6.2b. These results are compatible with those acquired in the previous section. The high-frequency noise content in the reconstruction, which is easily perceived in the profile, is undesirable. To improve the quality of the reconstruction, we switch to representation II for the contours. We now obtain the result shown in part c of Fig. 6.2, with the horizontal profile in part d. As is seen, the noise is greatly diminished by compressing the line patterns along which the projection data are collected.

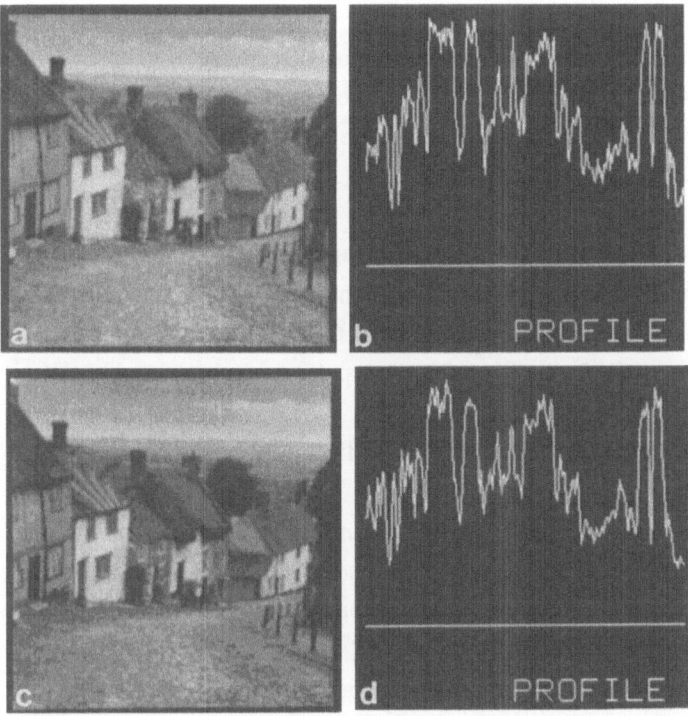

Fig. 6.2. Reconstruction via filtered backprojection (a), with profile (b), and reconstruction using representation II for linear contours (c), with profile (d)

6.2 Iterative Reconstruction

In iterative reconstruction techniques, also known as algebraic reconstruction techniques (ART), the reconstruction problem is formulated as a general image restoration problem, and is solved as a set of simultaneous linear equations [Gord74]. The *Kacmarz method* [Rose82] is one such technique.

6.2.1 The Kacmarz Method

Given a set of known projections for an image, the Kacmarz method for image reconstruction may be stated as follows:

1. Start with an arbitrary initial image.
2. For the current θ, take the projection of the image and subtract it from the known projection to obtain an array of correction values.
3. Backtrace the correction values over the image.
4. Increment θ, and go to step (2).

In this manner, one iterates around the image until it converges to the solution.[7] As stated, this algorithm is implemented as an unconstrained ART. One may also implement this algorithm as a partially constrained ART, in which the image resulting from step (3) is constrained to be all positive. We have experimented with both variations, and have found that the positivity constraint usually expedites the convergence of the algorithm.

The iterative nature of this algorithm implies two undesirable consequences. First, the rate of convergence is slow. In some cases, using 180 orientations spaced 1° apart, up to 20 passes around the image were necessary to provide a satisfactory solution (although in some cases, only 5 passes were sufficient). Second, the algorithm is not at all suited for pipelined implementation between orientations. The correction factor at one orientation must be completely backtraced before the projection is taken at the next orientation, so that the processing at one orientation cannot be pipelined with that at the next. There has been a different form of ART proposed, in which an iteration consists of computing correction factors at every orientation simultaneously, and backtracing them all at once. This technique is known as a *simultaneous algebraic reconstruction technique* (SIRT) [Gilb72a]. Unfortunately, the rate of convergence of this type of algorithm is extremely slow, and what one gains in the ability to pipeline, one loses in the number of iterations one must make.

Nevertheless, using a single P^3E stage, we can support the Kacmarz method. Although it would certainly not qualify as a real-time algorithm, we feel that our model and our architecture provide a feasible engine for a reasonably *fast* implementation. One advantage of our approach over

---

7 Convergence can be shown, and the limiting point is the image closest to the initial guess, in the mean-square norm sense, whose projections coincide with the given data.

conventional approaches lies, once again, in our representation for digital lines. We do not have to weight the individual pixel contributions to a contour by their fractional area contained in the contour, since this fraction is always 0 or 1 (this model for image reconstruction was first proposed by Gordon et al. in [Gord74]).

Part a of Fig. 6.3 shows a binary image, with a horizontal profile in part b. Using the Kacmarz method with the positivity constraint, and starting with an all-black image, the reconstruction after five passes around the image is shown in part c, with the corresponding profile in part d.

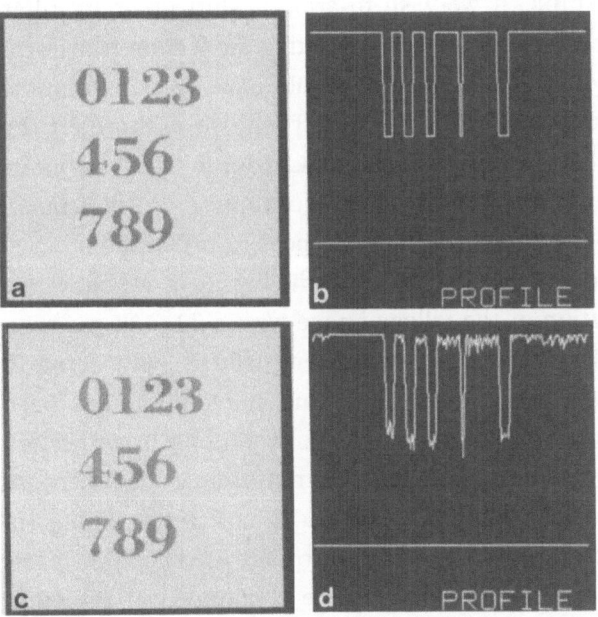

Fig. 6.3. Binary image (a), with horizontal profile (b), and reconstruction via iterative Kacmarz method (c), with profile (d)

6.3 Two-Dimensional Convolution

The Radon transform is useful for reducing the dimensionality of certain image processing operations. An example is the 2-D convolution of an image I with a large kernel K. A result from Radon theory states that:

$$^{\{I*K\}}P_\theta(t) = {^{\{I\}}}P_\theta(t) \ast {^{\{K\}}}P_\theta(t) \tag{6.3}$$

where ${}^{\{I*K\}}P_\theta(t)$ denotes the projection of the 2-D convolution $I*K$ at orientation θ, ${}^{\{I\}}P_\theta(t)$ denotes the projection of the image I at orientation θ, and likewise ${}^{\{K\}}P_\theta(t)$ denotes the projection of the K at orientation θ. This formula is referred to as the *convolution theorem*. It follows directly from the *Fourier slice theorem*[Rose82], or *projection slice theorem*, which equates a 1-D slice of an image's Fourier transform (at orientation θ through the origin) to the Fourier transform of the projection of the image at the same orientation.

The convolution theorem makes the powerful statement that a 2-D convolution in image space may be obtained as a series of 1-D convolutions in Radon space. For example, if we wish to apply a shift-invariant filter K to a digital image I, we may proceed by computing the Radon transform of I and K, and convolving the 1-D signals so obtained (which amounts to one convolution per angle in Radon space). Then, we backproject the filtered Radon transform to recover the filtered image $I*K$. It is interesting to remark that this method allows one to apply *multi-directional filters* to images by varying the kernel with respect to orientation.

To demonstrate the convolution theorem, in Fig. 6.4a we show the two-dimensional convolution of the village image with a 32×32 gaussian kernel, with $\sigma \cong 5$ pixels. This image has been padded with zeros to eliminate border effects. In Fig. 6.4c, the same convolution has been accomplished as a series of one-dimensional convolutions in projection space followed by backprojection. This image is not zero-padded, because the border effects have been eliminated by adequate zero-padding in projection space. For comparison, horizontal profiles are shown in parts b and d of Fig. 6.4. Note that the first profile is chopped at the ends, due to the zero-padding of the image in part a. As a second example, Fig. 6.4e shows the projection-space convolution of the village image with the well-known Marr-Poggio operator [Marr80] ($\sigma \cong 5$ pixels).

6.4 Rotation and Translation

Several elementary graphics transformations may also be applied to images in Radon space. One simple example is that of rotation: in projection space rotation corresponds to shifting the orientation of the projection

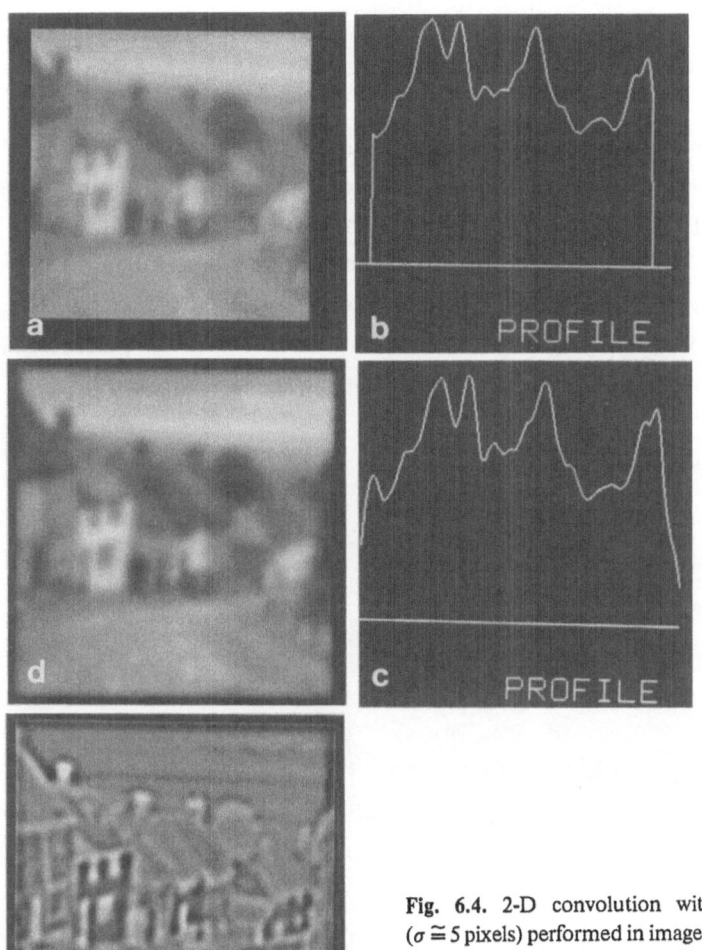

Fig. 6.4. 2-D convolution with 32×32 Gaussian ($\sigma \cong 5$ pixels) performed in image space (a), with profile (b), same convolution performed in projection space (c), with profile (d), and 2-D convolution with Marr-Poggio operator ($\sigma \cong 5$ pixels), performed in projection space (e)

arrays. The projection data remain unchanged. Another slightly more complicated example is that of translation. In this case, the data within each projection must be shifted according to the magnitude and direction of translation. The combined operations of rotation and translation are neatly represented in the following formula, which is used to derive the transformed projections $P_\theta'(t)$ from the originals:

$$P_\theta'(t) = P_{\theta-\alpha}[t - \sqrt{x_1^2 + y_1^2}\cos(\gamma - \theta)] \tag{6.4}$$

where the image is rotated counterclockwise by the angle α, and translated by an amount (x_1, y_1). γ is the direction of translation, i.e., $\gamma = \tan^{-1}(y_1 / x_1)$.

Due to the noise introduced by our digital model, this method of image rotation and translation will certainly not compete with conventional graphics techniques. However, as an academic exercise, the experiments we ran proved to be interesting. Fig. 6.5a shows the village image rotated by 60°, and Fig. 6.5b shows the same image translated 64 pixels to the right and 64 pixels down. These transformations were both performed in projection space, using the above equation.

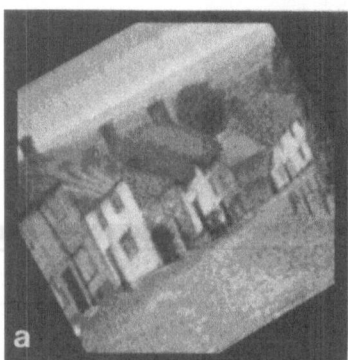 

Fig. 6.5. 60° rotation (a) and (64,64) translation (b) of village image performed in projection space

6.5 Computerized Tomography Reconstruction

Of great interest is to see how our model performs reconstruction from exact sampled-continuous projection data, which is analogous to parallel-beam CT data. With sampled-continuous projection data we are isolating the performance of the reconstruction process from the effects of digital projection-related noise. Thus, we can identify where the real limitations lie in our model.

To this end, we simulated parallel-beam data for the Shepp and Logan head phantom image, as shown in Fig. 6.6a, and described in Sect. 2.3. We then compared the reconstructions obtained using both digital projection data and the simulated CT data. In part b of Fig. 6.6,

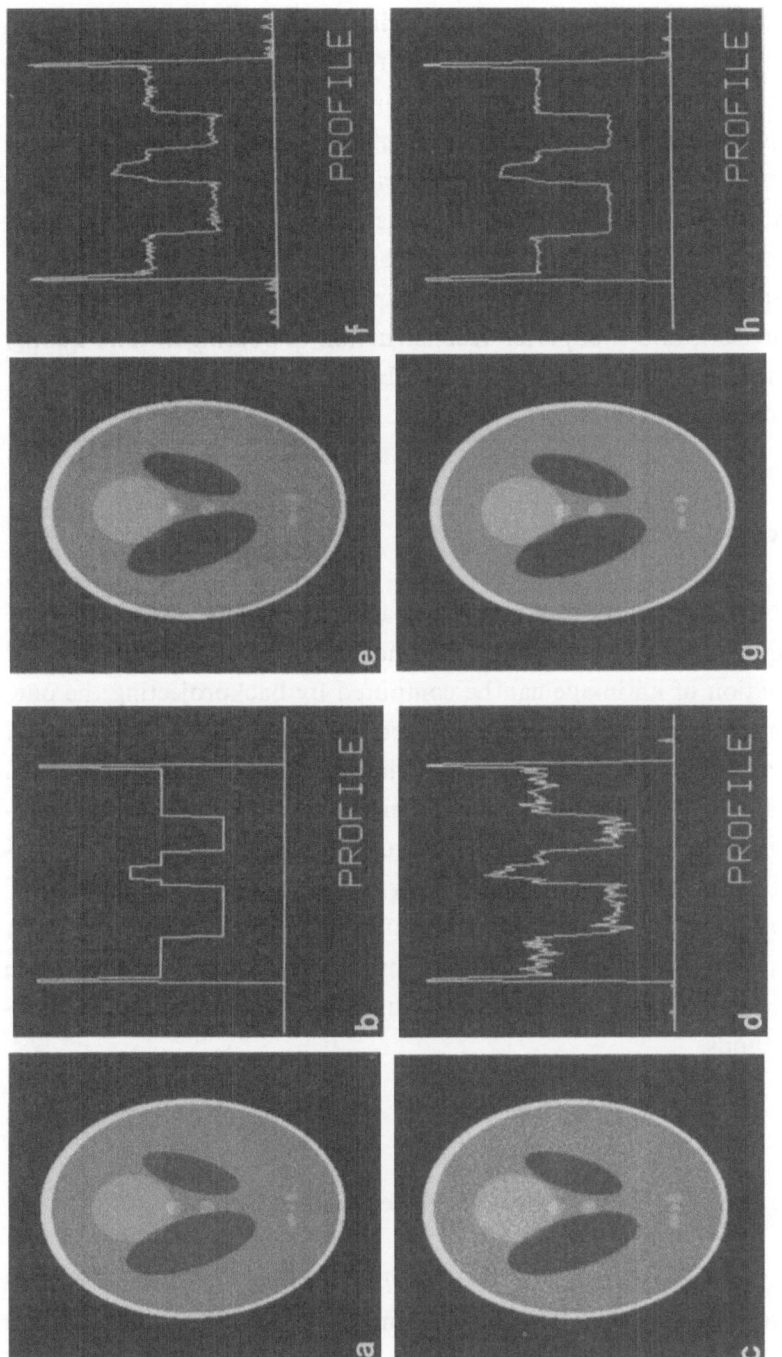

Fig. 6.6 Shepp and Logan "head phantom" image (**a**), with profile (**b**), reconstruction from digital projection data using representation I (**c**), with profile (**d**), reconstruction from digital projection data using representation II (**e**), with profile (**f**), and reconstruction from exact projection data using representation I (**g**), with profile (**h**)

we show a horizontal profile of the original image. The reconstruction obtained using digital projection data and representation I for the contours is shown in part c, with the corresponding profile in part d. The reconstruction is markedly noisy. Substantial improvement is gained by switching to representation II, as shown in parts e and f, although some high frequency noise remains. In contrast, the reconstruction obtained using exact data and representation I for the contours is shown in part g, with the corresponding profile in part h. As expected, even less high frequency noise is present, and a superior reconstruction is obtained. The quality of this image is comparable to that obtained using conventional CT reconstruction techniques.

6.6 Autocorrelation

The Radon representation of an image also allows one to decouple the computation of autocorrelations. In other words, the two-dimensional autocorrelation of an image can be computed by backprojecting the one-dimensional autocorrelation of the projections of the image. The proof of this property is similar to that of two-dimensional convolution, as in Sect. 6.3. The implementation of the one-dimensional correlations for the projection data can be accomplished by usual methods in the time or frequency domain. As an example, we show in part a of Fig. 6.7 an original image, and in parts b and d the computation of the autocorrelation by the direct and projection-based methods, respectively. The profiles in parts c and e illustrate the comparative quality of the exact and projection-based methods.

6.7 Polar Fourier Transform and Object Classification

As a direct consequence of the *Fourier slice theorem* (see Sect. 6.3), P^3E can be used to generate 2-D DFT's of images on polar rasters. Once a projection of an image is obtained for a certain angle, taking the DFT of that projection yields approximated polar samples of a central slice at

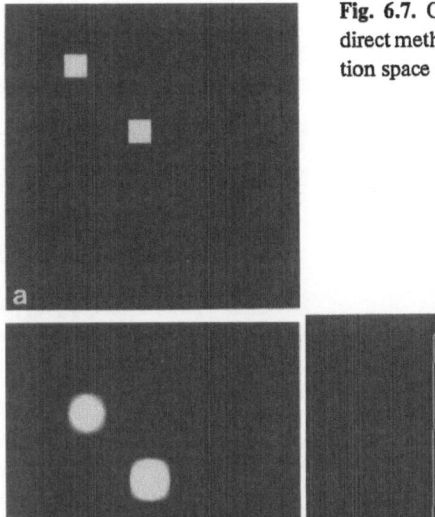

Fig. 6.7. Original image (**a**), autocorrelation obtained using direct method (**b**) with profile (**c**), and autocorrelation in projection space (**d**) with profile (**e**)

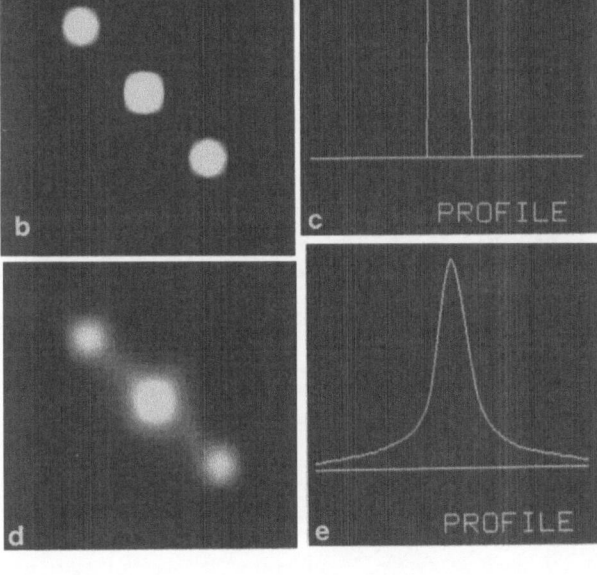

the same orientation of the 2-D Fourier transform of the image. The advantage of this approach over classical methods is that it does not require complicated interpolation techniques to map a discrete function from cartesian to polar coordinates. Also, it has a lower complexity than other methods based on generalizations of the Hankel transform.

Having polar Fourier transform data enables one to compute image features that are invariant to rotation and translation. These features can be obtained by circular harmonic expansions of the Fourier transform values on each circle centered at the origin. At present we are investigating the use of these features for object classification.

7. Radon Transform Theory for Random Fields and Optimum Image Reconstruction from Noisy Projections

Reconstruction from Noisy Projections/ In this chapter we present some recent results on Radon transform theory for stationary random fields. Specifically, we present a projection theorem which gives the relation between the power spectrum density of one-dimensional projections of a stationary random field and its two-dimensional power spectrum density. This result yields the optimum mean square reconstruction filter from noisy projections and is useful in other problems such as multi-dimensional spectral estimation from one-dimensional projections, noise analysis in computed tomography, etc.

7.1 Radon Transform Theory of Random Fields

Radon transform theory has been developed extensively for deterministic functions but little work has been done for random fields. One reason might be due to the fact that a fine integral of a stationary random field does not exist in the mean square sense. However, it can be shown that this integral is a singularity which can be expressed in terms of a Dirac delta function. This will allow us to study the stochastic properties of Radon transform of stationary random fields. Before further discussion, we will define various operators to simplify notation. First, we will denote the Radon transform of a two-dimensional $f(x,y)$ as $g(s, \theta)$, and the two will be related by the Radon transform operator R as follows:

$$g(s, \theta) \stackrel{\Delta}{=} Rf = \int_{-\infty}^{\infty} f(x,y)\, \delta(s - x\cos\theta - y\sin\theta)\mathrm{d}x\mathrm{d}y,$$

$$-\infty < s < \infty,\ 0 < \theta < \pi \tag{7.1}$$

The inverse Radon transform is given by

$$f(x,y) = \int_0^\pi \int_{-\infty}^\infty |\xi| \, G(\xi,\theta) \exp[j2\pi\xi(x\cos\theta + y\sin\theta)]dxdy \qquad (7.2)$$

where $G(\xi,\theta)$ is the one-dimensional (1-D) Fourier transform of $g(s,\theta)$ w.r.t. s. We will write this in operator notation as

$$f(x,y) \triangleq B\hat{g} = \int_0^\pi \hat{g}(x\cos\theta + y\sin\theta, \theta)d\theta \qquad (7.3)$$

$$\hat{g}(s,\theta) \triangleq Hg = \int_{-\infty}^\infty g(s',\theta)h(s-s')ds' \qquad (7.4)$$

where the operator B is the adjoint of R, and H is a convolution operator whose frequency response is $|\xi|$. In operator notation, we can now write:

$$g = Rf, \qquad R^{-1} = BH \qquad (7.5)$$

As an additional note, the *projection slice theorem* (mentioned in Sect. 6.3) states that $G(\xi,\theta)$ is the central slice at angle θ of $F(\xi_1,\xi_2)$, the two-dimensional Fourier transform of $f(x,y)$, i.e.,

$$G(\xi,\theta) = F(\xi\cos\theta, \xi\sin\theta) \qquad (7.6)$$

where (ξ,θ) are the polar coordinates in the spatial frequency plane defined by (ξ_1, ξ_2).

Now we can proceed by defining the linear operator $\tilde{R}$ which is a Radon transform followed by a 1-D convolution operator $H^{1/2}$ whose frequency response is $|\xi|^{1/2}$:

or
$$\tilde{R} \triangleq H^{1/2}R \qquad (7.7)$$

or
$$\tilde{g}(s,\theta) \triangleq \tilde{R}f = \int_{-\infty}^\infty |\xi|^{1/2}F(\xi\cos\theta, \xi\sin\theta)\exp(-j2\pi\xi s)d\xi \qquad (7.8)$$

or
$$\tilde{G}(\xi,\theta) = |\xi|^{1/2}G(\xi,\theta) = |\xi|^{1/2}F(\xi\cos\theta, \xi\sin\theta) \qquad (7.9)$$

This operator, although recognized in [Ludw66], is not widely known in the image reconstruction literature. It is equivalent to a 2-D high frequency emphasis filter followed by the Radon transform. This means we can also write

$$\tilde{g}(s,\theta) = R\tilde{f} = \int_{-\infty}^{\infty} \tilde{f}(x,y)\,\delta(s - x\cos\theta - y\sin\theta) \qquad (7.10)$$

where $\tilde{f}(x,y)$ is the output of the 2-D filter with frequency response $(\xi_1^2 + \xi_2^2)^{1/4}$. We can now state some useful properties of the transform $\tilde{R}$.

Theorem 1: The $\tilde{R}$-transform is unitary, i.e., $\tilde{R}^{-1} = \tilde{R}^*$, where $*$ denotes the adjoint. Moreover, it satisfies the energy conservation formula

$$\int_{-\infty}^{\infty}\int |f(x,y)|^2 dx dy = \int_{0}^{\pi}\int_{-\infty}^{\infty} |\tilde{g}(s,\theta)|^2 ds d\theta \qquad (7.11)$$

Now we consider some stochastic properties of the $\tilde{R}$-transform. Let $f(x,y)$ be a stationary random field with power spectrum density $S(\xi_1,\xi_2)$ and autocorrelation function $r(\tau_1,\tau_2)$. The corresponding functions for $\tilde{f}(x,y)$ will be $\tilde{S}(\xi_1,\xi_2) \stackrel{\Delta}{=} \sqrt{\xi_1^2 + \xi_2^2}\,S(\xi_1,\xi_2)$ and $\tilde{r}(\tau_1,\tau_2) = F_2^{-1}\{\tilde{S}(\xi_1,\xi_2)\}$. In polar coordinates we denote $S(\xi_1,\xi_2)$ by $S_p(\xi,\theta)$, and we define $r_p(s,\theta) \stackrel{\Delta}{=} F_1^{-1}\{S_p(\xi,\theta)\}$, $\forall\,\theta$. For simplicity in what follows, our treatment will be somewhat formal. More rigorous development via generalized Fourier theory is possible, and will be considered elsewhere. From the projection slice theorem, we can write $r_p(s,\theta) = Rr$.

1) Cross-Correlations

Using (7.10) it can be shown that

$$r_{\tilde{f}\tilde{g}}(x,y;s,\theta) \stackrel{\Delta}{=} E[\tilde{f}(x,y)\tilde{g}(s,\theta)] = \tilde{r}_p(s - x\cos\theta - y\sin\theta) \qquad (7.12)$$

where

$$\tilde{r}_p(s,\theta) = F_1^{-1}\{|\xi|\,S_p(\xi,\theta)\} \qquad (7.13)$$

$$r_{f\tilde{g}}(x,y;s,\theta) \stackrel{\Delta}{=} E[f(x,y)\tilde{g}(s,\theta)]$$
$$= [F_1^{-1}\{|\xi|^{1/2}S_p(\xi,\theta)\}](s - x\cos\theta - y\sin\theta) \qquad (7.14)$$

$$r_{fg}(x,y;s,\theta) \stackrel{\Delta}{=} E[f(x,y)g(s,\theta)] = r_p(s - x\cos\theta - y\sin\theta) \qquad (7.15)$$

89

Thus, the above cross correlations are constant along the paths of integration for projection at (s, θ).

2) Autocorrelations of $\tilde{g}$ and g

From (7.10,13) we can write

$$r_{\tilde{g}\tilde{g}}(s, \theta; s', \theta') = \int\int\limits_{-\infty}^{\infty} r_{\tilde{f}\tilde{g}}(x, y; s', \theta')\, \delta(s - x\cos\theta - y\sin\theta)dxdy$$

$$= \int\int\int\limits_{-\infty}^{\infty} |\xi| S_p(\xi, \theta)\exp\{j2\pi\xi(s' - x\cos\theta' - y\sin\theta')\} \cdot$$

$$\delta(s - x\cos\theta - y\sin\theta)dxdyd\xi$$

$$= \int\limits_{-\infty}^{\infty} |\xi| S_p(\xi, \theta)e^{j2\pi\xi s'} \alpha(s, \theta; \xi, \theta')d\xi$$

where $\alpha(s, \theta; \xi, \theta')$ is the Radon transform of the plane wave $\exp\{-j2\pi\xi(x\cos\theta' + y\sin\theta')\}$ and can be shown to be given by

$$\alpha(s, \theta; \xi, \theta') = \frac{1}{|\xi|}\exp(-j2\pi\xi s)\,\delta(\theta - \theta')$$

This gives the interesting result

$$r_{\tilde{g}\tilde{g}}(s, \theta; s', \theta') = r_p(s - s', \theta)\,\delta(\theta - \theta'); \quad r_p(s, \theta) \overset{F_1}{\longleftrightarrow} S_p(\xi, \theta) \quad (7.16)$$

which states that the filtered projections $\tilde{g}(x, \theta)$ are stationary in s and are uncorrelated in θ. This means $\tilde{R}$ is a whitening transform in θ for stationary random fields. Now, for each θ, if we define the one-dimensional power spectrum density $S_{\tilde{g}}(\xi, \theta)$ of $\tilde{g}(s, \theta)$ to be the 1-D Fourier transform of its autocorrelation $r_p(s, \theta)$, then

$$S_{\tilde{g}}(\xi, \theta) \overset{\Delta}{=} F_1\{r_p(s, \theta)\} = S_p(\xi, \theta) = S(\xi\cos\theta, \xi\sin\theta) \quad (7.17)$$

Equations (7.16,17) yield the following useful theorems.

Theorem 2: The operator $\tilde{R}$ is a whitening transform in θ for stationary random fields.

Corollary: The Radon transform is also a whitening transform in the variable θ for stationary random fields.

90

This follows due to the fact that $\tilde{R}$ and R are related by a linear transformation $H^{1/2}$ which is independent of θ.

Theorem 3: (Projection Slice Theorem for Random Fields). The one-dimensional power spectrum density $S_{\tilde{g}}(\xi, \theta)$ of the $\tilde{R}$-transform of a stationary random field $f(x,y)$ is the central slice at angle θ of the two-dimensional power spectrum density $S(\xi_1, \xi_2)$ of $f(x,y)$.

Corollary: From the relation between $\tilde{R}$ and R, it follows that

$$E[g(s, \theta)g(s', \theta')] = r_g(s - s', \theta)\, \delta(\theta - \theta') \qquad (7.18)$$

where

$$r_g(s, \theta) \overset{F_1}{\longleftrightarrow} S_g(\xi, \theta) = \frac{1}{|\xi|} S_p(\xi, \theta)$$

Remarks

1) Theorems 2 and 3 follow directly from (7.16,17), respectively.

2) Theorem 3 states that it is the 1-D power spectrum of $\tilde{g}(s, \theta)$ (the $\tilde{R}$-transform of f) and not of $g(x, \theta)$ (the R-transform of f) which is a slice of the 2-D power spectrum of $f(x,y)$.

3) The above result can be useful in estimating the two-dimensional power spectrum $S(\xi_1, \xi_2)$ from the projections of the random field sample functions. For example, if the usual projection data $g(s, \theta)$ are known, then one-dimensional spectral estimation techniques can be used to estimate $S_g(\xi, \theta)$, from which the 2-D power spectrum can be obtained as

$$\hat{S}_p(\xi, \theta) = S(\xi \cos \theta, \xi \sin \theta) = |\xi|\, S_g(\xi, \theta)$$

Alternatively, $g(s, \theta)$ can be filtered first to yield $\tilde{g}(s, \theta)$, from which $S_{\tilde{g}}$ can be estimated.

7.2 Optimum Reconstruction from Noisy Projections

The above results can be useful in optimum mean square estimation of an object from noisy and blurred projections, observed as

$$z(s, \theta) = \int_{-\infty}^{\infty} h(s - t, \theta)g(t, \theta)dt \ + \ \eta(s, \theta) \tag{7.19}$$

where $h(s, \theta)$ is the point spread function (PSF) of the imaging system and $\eta(s, \theta)$ is additive noise uncorrelated in θ, i.e.,

$$E[\eta(s, \theta)\eta(s', \theta')] = r_\eta(s - s', \theta) \ \delta(\theta - \theta'); \quad r_\eta(s, \theta) \overset{F_1}{\longleftrightarrow} S_\eta(\xi, \theta)$$

We also assume that η is uncorrelated with f and hence with g. The optimum linear mean square estimator would be of the form

$$\hat{f}(x, y) = \int_0^\pi \int_{-\infty}^\infty a(x, y; s, \theta)z(s, \theta)dsd\theta$$

The associated orthogonality condition together with (7.15,18) can be shown to yield

$$a(x, y; s, \theta) = a_p(s - x \cos \theta, y \sin \theta, \theta) \tag{7.20}$$

where

$$a_p(s, \theta) \overset{F_1}{\longleftrightarrow} A_p(\xi, \theta) \triangleq \frac{|\xi| H^*(\xi, \theta)S_p(\xi, \theta)}{|H(\xi, \theta)|^2 S_p(\xi, \theta) + |\xi| S_\eta(\xi, \theta)} \tag{7.21}$$

This gives

$$f(x, y) = \int_0^\pi \int_{-\infty}^\infty z(s, \theta)a_p(s - x \cos \theta - y \sin \theta)dsd\theta = BA_\theta z \tag{7.22}$$

which is, surprisingly, a filtered backprojection algorithm, where A_θ is the filtering operator whose frequency response is $A_p(\xi, \theta)$. Note that the filter $A_p(\xi, \theta)$ also depends on θ. Using (7.18) in (7.21) we obtain

$$A_p(\xi, \theta) = \frac{|\xi| H^* S_g}{|H|^2 S_g + S_\eta} \triangleq |\xi| W(\xi, \theta) \tag{7.23}$$

In the absence of blur (i.e., $H = 1$), we get

$$A_p(\xi, \theta) = \frac{|\xi| S_g(\xi, \theta)}{S_g(\xi, \theta) + S_\eta(\xi, \theta)} = \frac{|\xi|}{1 + \dfrac{S_\eta(\xi, \theta)}{S_g(\xi, \theta)}} \qquad (7.24)$$

Remarks

1) Note that $W(\xi, \theta)$ is the Wiener filter for each projection considered independently. Therefore, the global optimum reduces to a cascade of the (local) optimum linear filter for each projection followed by the (usual) inverse Radon transform.

2) Previous attempts [Cho77, Tsui79, Tsui78] to find the optimum linear random mean square filter for blurred and/or noisy Radon transform observations have generally yielded erroneous results because of their implicit assumption that $S_p(\xi, \theta)$ equals $S_g(\xi, \theta)$. Although the filter form of (7.21) can be obtained by first finding the optimum two-dimensional filter which should follow R^{-1}, and then combining a slice of that filter with $|\xi|$ [Tsui78], Theorem 3 (and hence (7.18)) is necessary to determine the filter of (7.23). This form of the filter is useful because in practice it may be desirable (or easier) to estimate $S_g(\xi, \theta)$ from $z(s, \theta)$, especially if the power spectrum of the object is expected to change significantly with θ.

8. Machine Vision Techniques for Visual Inspection

Some of the above algorithms, together with the P^3E architecture, can be used in real-world industrial applications. The most obvious case is that of non-destructive testing using CT reconstruction, as was shown in Sect. 6.5. However, there are other uses of P^3E such as *automated visual inspection*. In this chapter, we will describe the application of P^3E-based machine vision algorithms to automated visual inspection of *thin-film disk-heads*. A common experience in industrial applications of computer vision is that the problem of finding a set of image processing and image analysis algorithms *cannot* be separated from that of searching for a suitable architecture. In early studies, we estimated that a pipeline architecture should be appropriate for the inspection of thin-film heads. Having this possibility in mind, we tried to find algorithms amenable to raster-scan implementation.

As in many other problems involving image interpretation and description, our system for visual inspection of thin-film heads consists of modules divided into the following three basic categories:

- Image-to-image operations
- Image-to-symbol transformations
- Classification of symbolic objects

In the context of industrial visual inspection problems, the first group above is devoted to image pre-processing operations such as noise removal by multiple frame averaging, or shading correction to compensate for non-uniformities in the imaging process. On the other hand, the second and third groups attempt to identify defects in manufactured parts and to classify them according to prescribed engineering specifications.

Any realistic problem in the area of industrial machine vision involves smart sensing technology. The rationale for our choice of sensing devices which are suitable for thin-film heads lies beyond the scope of this discussion. It is enough for the purpose of this manuscript to say that we have chosen for the first prototype conventional darkfield and brightfield microscopy, followed by a TV camera. Images are then digitized into $512 \times 512 \times 8$ bits.

The main algorithms which are used in our digital system can be summarized as follows:

- Shading correction of brightfield and darkfield imagery
- Part location and boundary fitting
- Multi-color mask generation
- Thresholding and segmentation of brightfield and darkfield images
- Component labeling and feature extraction of potential defects
- Classification of defects
- Comparison with engineering specifications

The first five algorithms have been successfully implemented in general purpose image analysis pipeline architectures. The classification and comparison with specs are performed in a conventional microprocessor-based computer which hosts the pipeline architecture. The reasoning behind this breakdown in terms of algorithms vs. architectures is that the first five algorithms are the most time-consuming, due to the amount of data involved, and therefore they require specialized hardware. The remaining two algorithms, on the other hand, are much less time-consuming, and are adequately handled by the host microprocessor.

In this chapter, we describe some of the above modules and the way we mapped these algorithms onto a pipeline architecture. This architecture is based on the ideas presented in early sections of this manuscript. Some of the remaining algorithms above involve standard image operators which, although amenable to pipeline implementation, are not based on projection transforms and representations. Nevertheless, the following

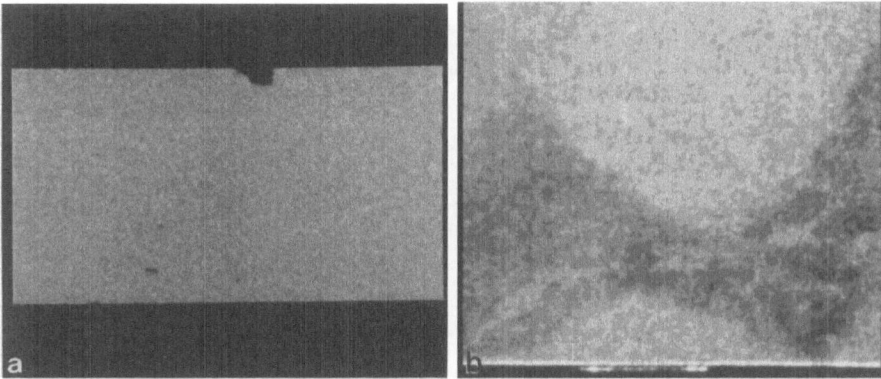

Fig. 8.1. Brightfield (a) and darkfield (b) images of disk heads

discussion provides a solid example of the utilization of a projection-based system for solving "real-world" industrial machine vision problems.

In Fig. 8.1a, we show a partial view (brightfield) of the air bearing surface of a thin-film head. The dark surface which surrounds the head rail is also subject to inspection. Some defects in this zone have poor reflection, and are therefore not imaged properly by this type of illumination. For that reason, we also use darkfield microscopy. In part b of Fig. 8.1, we show an image of the low-reflecting surface of the head, obtained by using an annular darkfield setting and the same resolution as in part a. The principle of darkfield microscopy is such that only scattered light is collected through the optical lenses. Since the low-reflecting black surface in question is rough, this illumination is suitable for imaging purposes. Figures 8.1a,b show different defects which require distinct analysis techniques. For example, the "chip" in part a is a boundary flaw whereas the defect in part b is a corruption of the normal texture of the surface produced by some deposited material. Other possible defects in the air bearing surfaces of disk-heads include voids, contaminants, abnormal graininess of the surface, scratches, etc..

There is also a good reason for utilizing both brightfield and darkfield for the *same* view of the part: using both of them aids in the design of a robust defect classification technique. Fig. 8.2a shows a brightfield image containing two different defects: contamination (dirt) and abnormal surface grain. In addition, Fig. 8.2b shows the same view but now using darkfield illumination. As is seen, the clear response of dirt to both

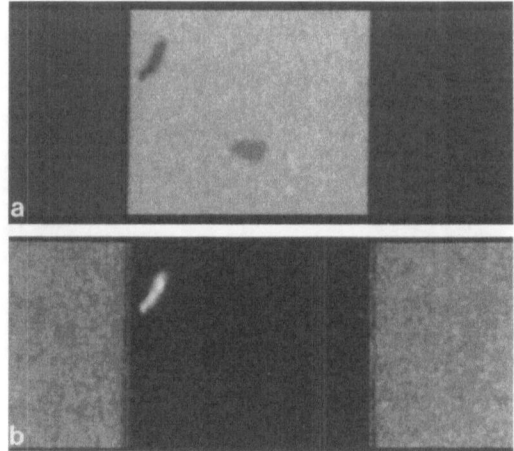

Fig. 8.2. Brightfield (a) and darkfield (b) images of disk heads

illuminations (which is not the case for the surface grain) yields the potential for having better discriminating gray-level features for classification purposes.

The images and discussion given above help create a reasonable impression of the complexity of this automated visual inspection problem. Specifically, the problem requires different illuminations with corresponding segmentation techniques, accompanied by shape analysis, defect discrimination, and pass/no-pass decision-making based on precise *contextual information* of defects. It also requires fast execution time. In order to keep the complexity of image segmentation to a minimum, we tried to simplify the job of the image analysis modules by presenting reasonable images to the system. Even under the best conditions, both darkfield and brightfield microscopy present *shading effects* due to non-uniformities in the response of the optics and camera. After linearizing the response of the imaging system to the light source, we can assume a linear pixel-by-pixel model for shading correcting the images [Petk85]. This correction is accomplished by the formula: $I_1(x,y) = [I(x,y) - B(x,y)]C(x,y)$, for all pixels (x,y), where B and C are the *bias* and the *correction factor* images, I is the input image and I_1 is the shading corrected image. In terms of computational requirements, the shading correction technique uses two fixed images B and C, which are computed only once (or periodically, depending on the degradation of illumination and optics). These images can be stored and utilized in a pipelined fashion that allows for raster implementation. Thus, the shading correction technique is amenable for fast pipeline implementation in P^3E.

The darkfield and brightfield images, compensated for their corresponding shading effects, are input to the image analysis modules. The brightfield image contains useful information involving the position and orientation of the disk-head as well as defects on its surface. The different reflectance properties of the materials allows for good visual discrimination of the boundaries of the rail and those between regions. There are two types of defects that we would like to detect and measure in brightfield imagery, namely defects identifiable by a distinguishing reflectance property (i.e., intensity in the gray-level image) and boundary defects (i.e., departures in the local or global geometry of the part). Since the part is made of different materials, there is a need for applying different detection techniques depending on the region being analyzed. For example, in Fig. 8.3a, defect detection in the light part at the bottom of the rail (which supports the bright read/write element) cannot be performed by the same decision process as in the textural area. Due to the application of shading correction techniques, and after experimenting with numerous samples, we concluded that a thresholding technique [Wezs78] could be used in brightfield images, and moreover, with the same threshold for all pixels in the given region. For the reasons explained above, the choice of the threshold should be based only on statistics collected from pixels of the same region.

There is also a need for detecting and *measuring* boundary flaws. For example, how much a chip intrudes into a given region and how much a protrusion departs from the normal geometry are typical *local measurements*. In addition, the width of the rail or the thickness of the read/write support zone are typical *global measurements*. Conventional shape analysis techniques, although they could eventually handle the detection of flaws, cannot measure the above parameters. Also, the actual extraction of the boundary pixels (as a necessary step for performing shape analysis) is a difficult task because of the noisy appearance of edges, and potential confusion with texture pixels. The complexity of this task has been well demonstrated by techniques such as those in [Neva76]. An alternative possibility for shape analysis and measurement is to ac-

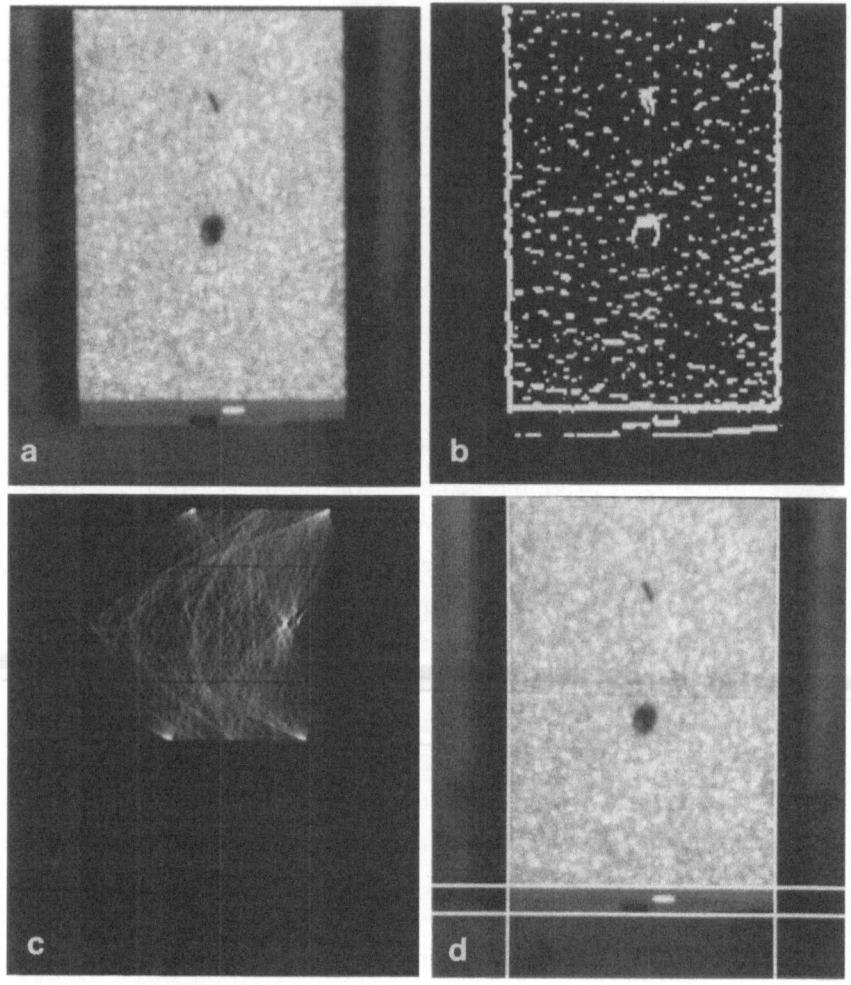

Fig. 8.3. (a) Brightfield image of disk head, (b) combined vertical and horizontal edge-maps of image in part a, (c) complete projection-space representation of gradient image in part b, and (d) detected edges overlaid on original image

tually fit an ideal boundary to the noisy edge data based on the fact that the shape of the disk-head is known apriori.[8]

The above reasons clearly indicate that performing a fitting of the boundaries according to a model of the disk head is a good approach. In this way, a physical segmentation between different materials can be

---

8 There are a variety of disk-head shapes to be handled. The one shown in Fig. 8.2 is a simple case. Other views, even of the same head, may present more complex shapes. Here we will concern ourselves only with the polygonal case.

obtained, allowing the application of individual thresholding techniques and effective measurement of boundary defects. The reader may wonder why the use of a fixed template is not attempted (at least a template that describes the correct geometry of the part for an ideal position and orientation). The fixed-template approach cannot be used for a variety of reasons, as will become clear in the following discussion. In fact, we are going to build a *reference* image but it will be based on data extracted from each part individually, and will consequently vary from part to part.

A maximum likelihood approach for parametric curves, such as the Hough transform, is a potential candidate for fitting edge points. Part b of Fig. 8.3 shows a gradient image, obtained by performing conventional local neighborhood edge detection on the image in part a. This gradient image is the combination of a thresholded vertical and a thresholded horizontal edge image. The noisy nature of this binary image will be compensated by following a global boundary fitting method. In a more general case, we run edge detectors sensitive to several other orientations. Also, the implementation should use the fact that some knowledge about the orientation and position of the disk-head in the field of view is available. For example, although the precise orientation is uncertain, the head can be constrained to lie within an interval of 5 degrees from the orientation shown in Fig. 8.3a. This means that not all possible values for the angle parameter of the Hough transform are necessary, but only those few orientations for which lines are expected in the image. A larger set of angles has to be spanned when tolerances in orientation are relaxed. By making P^3E long enough, many orientations of the Hough transform can be computed in a single pass if necessary.

The complete Hough transform for the gradient image of part b in Fig. 8.3 is shown in part c. The peaks correspond to the most likely positions of the four lines in the image. Note that the lower two peaks (at $\theta = 179°$) are actually part of the upper two (at $\theta = 0°$), since the projections for $\theta = 0°$ and $179°$ are very similar. The result of the Hough line-fitting process is shown in Fig. 8.3d, where the detected lines have been overlaid onto the original image.

It is clear that we have computed a geometrical template, which fits each disk-head in an optimal way according to the Hough transform. We can now differentiate between the areas defined by the lines, which correspond to different zones of interest. As we remarked above, the purpose of identifying these regions is two-fold: we need to determine which zones are affected by a defect and we must collect pixel statistics in each individual region for segmentation. In addition, the adaptive template mechanism yields a simple way to measure boundary defects. For example, a chip (which is a typical boundary defect) would be enclosed by its ideal boundary, and thus identified as a separate object from the background. We would then be able to compute its area, perimeter, and other meaningful features.

A good automated visual inspection tool should be capable of reporting all physical and engineering regions of an industrial part that a potential defect belongs to or touches. The computation of this *positional information* for defects can be greatly simplified by using multi-color mask images. Additionally, in image segmentation operations, it is common that different geometrical regions in the image should be processed individually. Depending on the particular architecture, this positional information can be efficiently represented and fed to the processor by means of an image which encodes different areas of interest. Each polygon determines an area which is to be separately checked for manufacturing defects. It is common that different regions have different quality-assurance engineering specifications. It is also common that these regions may not be given by different production materials but defined by functional properties of the parts. For example, in our disk-head problem it is necessary to check for defects in an area close to the read/write elements, or in other positions which are critical for flyability performance of the head. There is also another type of region which may be needed in automated inspection. This region relates to the specific image analysis tasks performed on the image. For example, we may not wish to apply a certain local operator indiscriminately on an image because of those areas which surround the physical boundary between materials of the part (for these pixels, unpredictable blurred results may occur). We will show an example of this situation for defect segmentation in darkfield imagery.

Although we have given some motivation for the use of digital polygonal masks in the visual inspection problem at hand, we also claim that these masks must be computed in real-time. Although the model is fixed for a given disk-head, the coded mask may *change* from part to part. The reasons are as follows:

— The actual dimensions of the disk-head may change slightly. Also, the relative position of the read/write element may change.
— The position and orientation of the disk-head (with respect to the background) under the imaging device may not be the same.

As was shown in Sect. 5.4, the P^3E approach to obtain this coloring in pipeline architectures is divided into two steps:

1. Create a digital *convex tesselation* of the plane by using the boundary lines found by the Hough transform and those corresponding to engineering-specified areas.
2. Reconstruct polygons (and segments) of interest by assigning the same code to each of their fractions in the tesselated image.

Figure 5.12 shows the result of the tesselation corresponding to the same part of a head as shown in Fig. 8.3a. The actual coloring of a polygon is obtained by a single look-up table operation on the tesselated image. For this purpose, one should know apriori the codes in the tesselated image which correspond to the polygon of interest. This information can be computed once and therefore off-line, since it does not vary from part to part. As an example, Fig. 8.4 shows a multi-color digital image for

Fig. 8.4. Multi-color disk head mask

some regions of interest in the same part of another head. As proof of the feasibility of this implementation in pipeline architectures, this image was computed in the same commercial processor as that of the other algorithms in this chapter.

After individual regions have been extracted, different segmentations techniques are applied to brightfield and darkfield images. The operations involved are amenable to pipeline implementations and they are based on global histogramming methods [Petk85, Sanz85]. Although these operations are easily supported by P^3E, they do not require projections, and hence will not be elaborated upon here. After applying the segmentation technique in each region, potential defects are detected as shown in Fig. 8.4. Of particular interest is the chip in the lower left portion of the head. Such an image would then be forwarded to a component labeling and feature extraction module, after which defects would be classified according to engineering specifications [Petk85].

9. Conclusion

We have demonstrated the completeness of our model for digital projections by showing that it supports a discrete version not only of the Radon transform, but also of the *inverse* Radon transform. We have also shown the feasibility of fast, real-time implementation of these operators through the use of a powerful pipeline architecture (P^3E), which supports a wide variety of projection-based image analysis and image processing tasks. We have surveyed and presented several image analysis and image processing algorithms that are easily mapped onto P^3E. We have shown favorable results for a variety of reconstruction techniques and applications.

The architecture we have proposed does indeed unleash the power of Radon theory for digital images. Our hope is that such computational tractability will encourage more widespread use of projection-based computer vision. Several issues remain to be studied. These include further reducing the effects of noise in the computation of projections, and experimenting with a number of potential yet unresolved vision applications for P^3E. Finally, we are pursuing the possible VLSI implementation of key P^3E components, which will be an important step toward its actual hardware realization.

Bibliography

[Ackl81]   B. Ackland, N. Weste, "The edge flag algorithm - A fill method for raster scan displays," *IEEE Trans. Comput.*, **C-30**, 1 (Jan. 1981).

[Akl79]   S. Akl, G. Toussaint, "Efficient convex hull algorithms for pattern recognition applications," *Proc. Fourth Int. Conf. on Pattern Recogn.*, Kyoto, Japan, 1979, pp. 483-487.

[Alts82]   M. Altschuler, Y. Censor, G. Herman, A. Lent, R. Lewitt, S. Srihari, H. Tuy, J. Udupa, "Mathematical aspects of image reconstruction from projections," Tech. Rep. No. MIPG70, Department of Radiology, University of Pennsylvania, 1982.

[Ande58]   W. Anderson, *An Introduction to Multivariate Statistical Analysis.* Wiley, New York 1958.

[Anto81]   D. Antonson et al., "PICAP - A System Approach to Image Processing," *Proc. IEEE Workshop on Computer Architectures for Pattern Analysis and Image Database Management*, Hot Springs, VA, Nov. 1981.

[Ball82]   D. Ballard, C. Brown, *Computer Vision.* Prentice Hall, Englewood Cliffs, NJ 1982.

[Bhat83]   B. K. Bhattacharya, G. Toussaint, "Time and storage efficient implementation of an optimal planar convex hull algorithm," *Image and Vision Computing*, **1**, 3 (Aug. 1983), pp. 140-144.

[Blan87]   W. E. Blanz, J. L. C. Sanz, E. B. Hinkle, "Image analysis methods for visual inspection of solder balls integrated circuit manufacturing," *IEEE Journal of Robotics and Automation*, in press.

[Brac79]   R. Bracewell, "Image reconstruction in radio astronomy," in *Image Reconstruction from Projections: Implementations and*

Applications, G. Herman, Ed. Springer-Verlag, New York 1979.

[Breu75] P. Breuer, M. Vajta, "Structural character recognition by forming projections," *Problems Control Inform. Theory* (Hungary), **4**, 4 (1975), pp. 339-352.

[Cant87] V. Cantoni, "I. P. hierchical systems: Architectural features," in *Pyramidal Systems for Computer Vision*, NATO Series, vol. 25, V. Cantoni, S. Levialdi, Eds. Springer-Verlag, New York 1987.

[Cant83] V. Cantoni, C. Guerra, S. Levialdi, "Toward an evaluation of an image processing system," in *Computing Structures for Image Processing*, M. J. B. Duff, Ed. Academic Press, London 1983.

[Cart86] H. W. Carter, "Computer-aided design of integrated circuits," *IEEE Computer*, Apr. 1986, pp. 19-36.

[Casa82] D. Casasent, L. Cheatham, D. Fetterly, "Hybrid optical-digital moment-based robotic pattern recognition system," *Proc. SPIE Int. Soc. Opt. Eng.*, **360** (1982), pp. 105-111.

[Chaz79] B. Chazelle, B. Dobkin, "Decomposing a polygon into its convex parts," *Proc. Eleventh A.C.M. Symposium on Theory of Computing*, Atlanta, GA, 1979.

[Cho77] Z. Cho and J. Burger, *IEEE Trans. Nucl. Sci.*, **NS-30**, 2 (Apr. 1977), pp. 886-893.

[Crow77] F. C. Crow, "Shadow algorithms for computer graphics," *A.C.M. SIGGRAPH Computer Graphics, Vol. 2 No. 1*, San Jose, CA, 1977.

[Cyph87] R. Cypher, J. L. C. Sanz, "SIMD mesh array algorithms for image component labeling," IBM Technical Report, Almaden Research Center, San Jose, CA, Feb. 1987.

[Dani81] P. E. Danielson, S. Levialdi, "Computer architectures for pictorial information processing," *IEEE Computer*, Nov. 1981, pp. 53-67.

[Davi84] Davis, Thomas, "Systolic array chip matches the pace of high-speed processing," *Electronic Design*, Oct. 31, 1984.

[Deva84]   A. Devaney, "Geophysical diffraction tomography," *IEEE Trans. Geosci. Remote Sensing*, Jan. 1984.

[Devr81]   L. Devroye, G. Toussaint, "A note on linear expected time algorithms for finding convex hulls," *Computing*, **26** (1981), pp. 361-366.

[Dist82]   A. Distante, N. Veneziani, "Two-pass filling algorithm for raster graphics," *Computer Graphics and Image Processing*, **20** (1982).

[Doug85]   R. Douglass, "A qualitative assessment of parallelism in expert systems," *IEEE Software*, May 1985, pp. 70-81.

[Duda72]   R. Duda, P. Hart, "Use of the Hough transform to detect lines and curves in pictures," *Comm. of the A.C.M.*, **15**, 1 (1972).

[Dudg84]   D. Dudgeon, R. Mersereau, *Multidimensional Digital Signal Processing*. Prentice Hall, Englewood Cliffs, NJ 1984.

[Duff76]   M. J. B. Duff, "CLIP4: A large scale integrated circuit array parallel processor," *Proc. Third Int. Conf. on Pattern Recogn.*, 1976, pp. 728-723.

[Dyer83]   C. Dyer, "Gauge inspection using Hough transform," *IEEE Trans. on Pattern Anal. and Mach. Intell.*, **PAMI-5**, 6 (Nov. 1983).

[Eddy77]   W. Eddy, "A new convex hull algorithm for planar sets," *A.C.M. Trans. Math. Software*, **3**, 4 (1977), pp.399-403, 411-412.

[Erma78]   L. Erman, V. Lesser, "System engineering techniques for artificial intelligence systems," in *Computer Vision Systems*, Hanson and Riseman, Eds. Academic Press, Orlando, FL 1978.

[Etch83]   D. Etchells, "A study of parallel architectures for image understanding algorithms," Image Understanding Research Technical Report, Department of Electrical Engineering and Computer Science, University of Southern California, ISG Rep. 104, Oct. 19, 1983.

[Feng72]   T. Feng, "Some characteristics of associative-parallel process-ing," *Proc. Sagamore Computer Conf.*, Syracuse University, 1972, pp. 5-16.

[Flyn66]   M. Flynn, "Very high computing systems," *Proc. IEEE*, **54** (1966), pp. 1901-1909.

[Foun86]   T. J. Fountain, "Array architectures for iconic and symbolic image processing," *Proc. Eighth Int. Conf. on Pattern Recogn.*, Paris, Oct. 1986.

[Foun85]   T. J. Fountain, "Plans for the CLIP7 chip," in *Integrated Technology for Parallel Image Processing*, S. Levialdi, Ed. Academic Press, London 1985.

[Foun83]   T. J. Fountain, "A survey of bit-serial processor circuits," in *Computing Structures for Image Processing*, M. J. B. Duff, Ed. Academic Press, London 1983.

[Fung77]   L. W. Fung, "A massively parallel processing computer," in *High-Speed Computer and Algorithm Organization*, D. J. Kuck et al., Eds. Academic Press, New York 1977.

[Fu81]   K. Fu, J. Mu, "A survey on image segmentation," *Pattern Recogn.*, **13** (1981).

[Gene85]   D. B. Genery, B. Wilcox, "A pipelined processor for low-level vision," *Proc. IEEE Conf. on Computer Vision and Pattern Recogn.*, San Francisco, 1985, pp. 608-613.

[Gilb72a]   P. Gilbert, "Iterative methods for the reconstruction of three dimensional objects from their projections," *J. Theoret. Biol.*, **36** (1972), pp. 105-117.

[Gilb72b]   P. Gilbert, "The reconstruction of three-dimensional structure from projections and its application to electron microscopy. II. Direct methods," *Proc. Roy. Soc. London Ser. B*, **182** (1972), pp. 89-102.

[Gord74]   R. Gordon, "A tutorial on ART (Algebraic Reconstruction Techniques)," *IEEE Trans. Nucl. Sci.*, **NS-21** (1974), pp. 78-93.

[Grim81]   W. Grimson, *From Images to Surfaces: A Computational Study of the Human Early Vision System*. M.I.T. Press, Cambridge, MA 1981.

[Jain87] W. Grosky, R. Jain, "A pyramid-based approach to segmentation applied to region matching," *IEEE Trans. Pattern Anal. Mach. Intell.*, **PAMI-8** (Sep. 1986).

[Gros85] T. Gross, H. T. Kung, M. Lam, J. Webb, "WARP as a machine for low-level vision," *Proc. IEEE Int. Conf. on Robotics and Automation*, Mar. 1985.

[Haen77] W. Haendler, *Proc. IEEE Int. Conf. on Parallel Processing*, 1977, pp. 7-15.

[Hara85] R. Haralick, "A reconfigurable systolic network for computer vision," *Proc. IEEE Workshop on Computer Architectures for Pattern Analysis and Image Database Management*, Miami, 1985.

[Heff82] P. B. Heffernan, R. H. T. Bates, "Image reconstruction from projections. VI: Comparison of interpolation methods," *Optik*, **60** (1982), pp. 129-142.

[Helg80] S. Helgason, *The Radon Transform*. Birkhauser, Boston, MA 1980.

[Herm80] G. Herman, *Image Reconstruction from Projections: The Fundamentals of Computerized Tomography*. Academic Press, New York 1980.

[Herm79] G. Herman, *Image Reconstruction from Projections: Implementation and Applications*. Springer-Verlag, Berlin 1979.

[Herm76] G. Herman, A. Lent, "Iterative reconstruction algorithms," *Comput. Biol. Med.*, **6** (1976), pp. 273-294.

[Herm73] G. Herman, "Reconstruction of binary patterns from a few projections," *Proc. International Computing Symposium*, Davos, Switzerland, Sep. 1973, pp. 371-379.

[Hild83] E. Hildreth, "The detection of intensity changes by computer and biological vision systems," *Computer Vision, Graphics and Image Processing*, **22** (1983), pp. 1-27.

[Hill85] D. Hillis, *The Connection Machine*. M.I.T. Press, Cambridge, MA 1985.

[Hink87] E. Hinkle, J. Sanz, A. Jain, D. Petkovic, "P^3E: New life for projection-based image processing," *Journal of Parallel and Distributed Computing*, **4** (1987), pp. 45-78.

[Ho83]   C. Ho, "Precision of digital vision systems," *IEEE Trans. Pattern Anal. Mach. Intell.*, **PAMI-5**, 6 (Nov. 1983), pp. 593-601.

[Hunt81]   D. J. Hunt, "The ICL DAP and its application for image processing," in *Languages and Architectures for Image Processing*, M. J. B. Duff, S. Levialdi Eds.   Academic press, London 1981.

[Hwan87]   K. Hwang, J. Ghish, R. Chowkwanyun, "Computer architectures for artificial intelligence processing," *IEEE Computer*, Jan. 1987.

[Hwan83]   K. Hwang, "Computer architectures for image processing," *IEEE Computer*, Jan. 1983.

[Ibra85]   H. Ibrahim, J. Kender, D. Elliot Shaw, "The analysis and performance of a two middle-level vision tasks on a fine-grained SIMD tree machine," *IEEE Conf. on Computer Vision and Pattern Recogn.*, San Francisco, 1985.

[Jain84]   A. Jain, S. Ansari, "Radon transform theory for random fields and optimum image reconstruction from noisy projections," *Proc. ICASSP '84*, San Diego.

[Jami86]   L. Jamieson, H. J. Siegel, E. J. Delp, A. Wonston, "The mapping of parallel algorithms to reconfigurable parallel architectures," *Proc. ARO Workshop on Future Directions in Computer Architecture and Software*, Charleston, SC, May 1986.

[Kash75]   R. Kashyap, M. Mittal, "Picture reconstruction from projections," *IEEE Trans. Comput.*, **C-24** (1975), pp. 915-923.

[Kent85]   E. Kent, S. Tanimoto, "Hierarchical cellular logic and the PIPE processor: Structural and functional correspondence," *Proc. IEEE Workshop on Computer Architectures for Pattern Analysis and Image Database Management*, Miami, 1985.

[Kibl85]   D. Kibler, J. Conery, "Parallelism in AI programs," *Proc. Ninth Int. Joint Conf. on Artificial Intelligence*, Los Angeles, 1985.

[Kimm85]   M. J. Kimmel, R. S. Jaffe, J. R. Mandeville, M. A. Lavin, "MITE : Morphic Image Transform Engine, an architecture for reconfigurable pipelines of neighborhood processors," *Proc. IEEE Workshop on Computer Architecture for Pattern Analysis and Image Database Management*, Miami, 1985.

[Kim82]   C. Kim, J. Sklansky, "Digital and cellular convexity," *Pattern Recogn.*, **15**, 5 (1982), pp. 359-367.

[Kim81]   C. Kim, "On the cellular convexity of complexes," *IEEE Trans. Pattern Anal. Mach. Intell.*, **PAMI-3** (1981), pp. 617-625.

[Lewi83] R. Lewitt, "Reconstruction algorithms: Transform methods," Tech. Rep. No. MIPG74, Department of Radiology, University of Pennsylvania, 1983.

[Lieb78] H. Lieberman, "How to color in a coloring book," *Computer Graphics*, **12** (Aug. 1978), pp. 111-116.

[Loug80] R. M. Lougheed, D. L. McCubberey, "The Cytocomputer: A practical pipelined image processor," *Proc. Seventh International Symposium on Computer Architecture*, La Boule, France, May 1980, pp. 271-277.

[Ludw66] L. Ludwig, *Commun. Pure Appl. Math.*, **19** (1966), pp. 49-81.

[Ma79]   Khe-ta Ma, G. Kusic, "An algorithm for distortion analysis in two-dimensional patterns using its projections," *Proc. Seventh New England Bioengineering Conf.*, Troy, N.Y. 1979, pp. 177-180.

[Marr82] D. Marr, *Vision*. Freeman, San Francisco 1982.

[Marr80] D. Marr, E. Hildreth, "Theory of edge detection," *Proc. Roy. Soc. London Ser. B*, **207** (1980), pp. 187-217.

[McCo63] B. H. McCormick, "The Illinois pattern recognition computer - ILLIAC III," *IEEE Trans. Comput.*, Dec. 1963, pp. 791-813.

[Mers74] R. Mersereau, A. Oppenheim, "Digital reconstruction of multidimensional signals from their projections," *Proc. IEEE*, **62** (1974), pp. 1319-1338.

[Meri87] A. Merigot, P. Clermonst, J. Mehat, F. Devos, B. Zavidovique, "A pyramidal system for image processing," in *Pyramidal Systems for Computer Vision*, NATO Series, vol. 25, V. Cantoni, S. Levialdi, Eds. Springer-Verlag, New York 1987.

[Muns84] D. C. Munson, J. L. C. Sanz, "Image reconstruction from frequency-offset Fourier data," *Proc. IEEE,* **72** (June 1984), pp. 661-669.

[Muns83] D. C. Munson, J. O'brien, K. W. Jenkins, "A tomographic formulation of spotlight mode synthetic aperture radar," *Proc. IEEE,* **71** (Aug. 1983), pp. 917-925.

[NCUB] NCUBE Corporation Product Report, NCUBE Corp. Headquarters, Beaverton, Oregon.

[Neva82] R. Nevatia, *Machine Perception.* Prentice Hall, Englewood Cliffs, NJ 1982.

[Neva78] R. Nevatia, "Characterization and requirements of computer vision systems," in *Computer Vision Systems,* Hanson and Riseman, Eds. Academic Press, Orlando, FL 1978.

[Neva76] R. Nevatia, "Locating object boundaries in textured environments," *IEEE Trans. Comput.,* Nov. 1976, pp. 1170-1175.

[Newm79] W. Newman, R. Sproull, *Principles of Interactive Computer Graphics.* McGraw-Hill, New York 1979.

[Offe85] R. J. Offen (Ed.), *VLSI Image Processing.* McGraw-Hill, New York 1985.

[Pave78] M. Pavel, "A unified setting for projections in pattern recognition," *Pattern Recogn.,* **10,** 4 (1978), pp. 249-254.

[Pavl78a] T. Pavlidis, "Algorithms for shape analysis of contours and waveforms," *Proc. Fourth Int. Conf. on Pattern Recogn.,* Kyoto, Japan, 1978, pp. 70-85.

[Pavl78b] T. Pavlidis, "Filling algorithms for raster graphics," Department of Electrical Engineering and Computer Science, Princeton University, Rep. No. 238, Jan. 1978.

[Petk85] D. Petkovic, J. Sanz, K. Mohiuddin, M. Flickner, E. Hinkle, C. Cox, K. Wong, "An experimental system for disk head inspection," Res. Rep. No. RJ-4942, IBM Almaden Research Center, San Jose, 1985.

[Prat78] W. K. Pratt, *Digital Image Processing.* Wiley, New York 1978.

[Ratt81]   P. Rattey, A. Lindgren, "Sampling the 2-D Radon transform," *IEEE Trans. Acoust., Speech, Signal Processing*, **29** (1981), pp. 994-1002.

[Ravi79]   J. Raviv, J. F. Greenleaf, G. T. Herman (Eds.), *Computer Aided Tomography and Ultrasonics in Medicine.* North-Holland, Amsterdam 1979.

[Redd78]   R. Reddy, "Pragmatic aspects of machine vision," in *Computer Vision Systems*, Hanson and Riseman, Eds. Academic Press, Orlando, FL 1978.

[Reev87]   A. P. Reeves, "Pyramid algorithms on processor arrays," in *Pyramidal Systems for Computer Vision*, NATO Series, vol. 25, V. Cantoni, S. Levialdi, Eds. Springer-Verlag, New York 1987.

[Reev84]   A. P. Reeves, "Survey: Parallel computer architectures for image processing," *Computer Vision, Graphics, and Image Processing*, **25** (1984), pp. 68-88.

[Reev83a] A. P. Reeves, "Fault tolerance in highly parallel mesh connected processors," in *Computing Structures for Image Processing*, M. J. B. Duff, Ed. Academic Press, London 1983.

[Reev83b] A. Reeves, B. Wittner, "Shape analysis of three dimensional objects using the method of moments," *Proc. IEEE Conf. on Computer Vision and Pattern Recogn.*, 1983, pp. 19-23.

[Rice85]   T. Rice, L. Jamieson, "Parallel processing for computer vision," in *Integrated Technology for Parallel Image Processing*, S. Levialdi, Ed. Academic Press, Orlando, FL 1985.

[Rieg81]   C. Rieger, "ZMOB: Doing it in parallel," *Proc. IEEE Workshop on Computer Architectures for Pattern Analysis and Image Database Management*, Hot Springs, VA, Nov. 1981, pp. 119-124.

[Robi82]   E. Robinson, "Spectral approach to geophysical inversion by Lorentz, Fourier, and Radon Transforms," *Proc. IEEE*, **70**, 9 (1982), pp. 1039-1054.

[Rose84]   A. Rosenfeld, "Image analysis: problems, progress and prospects," *Pattern Recogn.*, **17**, 1 (Jan. 1984), pp. 3-12.

[Rose82]   A. Rosenfeld, A. Kak, *Digital Picture Processing, Vol. I.* Academic Press, Orlando, FL 1982.

[Ruet86]   P. Ruetz, R. Brodersen, "A custom chip set for real-time image processing," *Proc. ICASSP '86*, San Jose.

[Sanz]   J. L. C. Sanz, J. W. Apffel, W. Sander, A. K. Jain, "Industrial Machine Vision," in *The Encyclopedia of Robotics*, in press. Wiley, New York.

[Sanz87a]   J. L. C. Sanz, I. Dinstein, D. Petkovic, "A new procedure for computing multi-colored polygonal masks in pipeline architectures and its application to automated visual inspection," *Commun. A.C.M.*, **30**, 4 (Apr. 1987), pp. 318-329.

[Sanz87b]   J. L. C. Sanz, E. Hinkle, I. Dinstein, "A new approach to computing geometrical features of digital objects for machine vision, image analysis and image processing: algorithms in pipeline architectures," *Proc. ICASSP '85*; also *IEEE Trans. Pattern Anal. Mach. Intell.*, **PAMI-9**, 1 (Jan. 1987), pp. 160-167.

[Sanz86a]   J. L. C. Sanz, A. K. Jain, "Machine vision methods for inspection of printed wiring boards and thick-Film circuits," *J. Opt. Soc. of America*, **3**, 9 (Sep. 1986), pp. 1465-1482.

[Sanz86b]   J. L. C. Sanz, D. Petkovic, K. Wong, "Image analysis algorithms for automated visual inspection of disk heads," in *Advances in Image Processing and Pattern Recognition*, V. Capellini, R. Marconi, Eds. North-Holland, Amsterdam 1986.

[Sanz85]   J. L. C. Sanz, F. Merkle, K. Wong, "Automated digital visual inspection with darkfield microscopy," *J. Opt. Soc. of America*, **2**, 11 (Nov. 1985), pp. 1857-1862.

[Scha78]   B. Schachter, "Decomposition of polygons into convex sets," *IEEE Trans. Comput.*, **C-27** (1978), pp. 1078-1082.

[Scha87]   D. Schaefer, P. Ho, "Counting on the GAM pyramid," in *Pyramidal Systems for Computer Vision*, NATO Series, vol. 25, V. Cantoni, S. Levialdi, Eds. Springer-Verlag, New York 1987.

[Sche83]   D. Scheibner, "The discrete Radon transform with some applications to velocity estimation," Department of Electrical Engineering, Rice University, Tech. Rep. No. 8301, 1983.

116

[Seit85]   C. Seitz, "The Cosmic Cube," *Commun. A.C.M.*, **28** (Jan. 1985).

[Sieg81]   H. J. Siegel et al., "PASM: A partitionable SIMD/MIMD system for image processing and pattern recognition," *IEEE Trans. Comput.*, **C-30** (1981).

[Silb85]   T. Silberberg, "The Hough transform on the Geometric Arithmetic Parallel Processor," *Proc. IEEE Workshop on Computer Architectures for Pattern Analysis and Image Database Management*, Miami, 1985.

[Skla82]   J. Sklansky, "Finding the convex hull of a simple polygon," *Pattern Recogn. Letters*, **1** (1982), pp. 79-83.

[Skla72]   J. Sklansky, "Measuring concavity on a rectangular mosaic," *IEEE Trans. Comput.*, **C-21** (1972), pp. 1355-1364.

[Skla70]   J. Sklansky, "Recognition of convex blobs," *Pattern Recogn.*, **2** (1970), pp. 3-10.

[Ster85]   S. Sternberg, "An overview of image algebra and related architectures," in *Integrated Technology for Parallel Image Processing*, S. Levialdi, Ed. Academic Press, Orlando, FL 1985.

[Ster79]   S. Sternberg, "Parallel architectures for image processing," *Proc. Third IEEE COMPSAC*, Chicago, 1979, pp. 712-717.

[Swee73]   D. W. Sweeney, C. M. Vest, "Reconstruction of three-dimensional refractive index fields from multi-directional interferometric data," *Appl. Opt.*, **12** (1973), pp. 1649-1664.

[Tana86]   H. Tanaka, "A parallel inference machine," *IEEE Computer*, **19**, 5 (May 1986), pp. 48-54.

[Tani87]   S. Tanimoto, "Paradigms for pyramid machine algorithms," in *Pyramidal Systems for Computer Vision*, NATO Series, vol. 25, V. Cantoni, S. Levialdi, Eds. Springer-Verlag, New York 1987.

[Tous83]   G. Toussaint, H. El Gindy, "A counterexample to an algorithm for computing monotone hulls of simple polygons," *Pattern Recogn. Letters*, May 1983, pp. 219-222.

[Tous80]   G. Toussaint, "Pattern recognition and geometrical complexity," *Proc. Fifth Int. Conf. on Pattern Recogn.*, Miami Beach, 1980, pp. 1324-1347.

[Tsui79]   E. T. Tsui, T. F. Budinger, *IEEE Trans. Nucl. Sci.*, **NS-26**, 2 (Apr. 1979), pp. 2687-2690.

[Tsui78]   E. T. Tsui, Ph.D. Dissertation, Dept. of Electrical Engineering and Computer Sciences, University of California, Berkeley, Nov. 1978.

[Uhr84]   L. Uhr, *Algorithm-structured computer arrays and networks.* Academic Press, Orlando, FL 1984.

[Uhr83]   L. Uhr, "Pyramid multi-computer structures, and augmented pyramids," in *Computing Structures for Image Processing*, M. J. B. Duff, Ed. Academic Press, London 1983.

[Veil78]   F. Veillon, "One pass computation of morphological and geometrical properties of objects in digital pictures," *Proc. Fourth Int. Conf. on Pattern Recogn.*, Kyoto, Japan, 1978, pp. 672-674.

[Vuyl81]   P. Vuylsteke, A. Oosterlinck, H. van der Berge, "Labelling and simultaneous feature extraction in one pass," *SPIE Vol. 301, Design of Digital Image Processing Systems*, 1981, pp. 173-180.

[Wah86]   B. Wah, G. Li, "Computers for artificial intelligence applications," IEEE Tutorial, ISBN-0-8186-0706-8, May 1986.

[Wang75]   Y. R. Wang, "Characterization of binary patterns and their projections," *IEEE Trans. Comput.*, **C-24**, 10 (Oct. 1975).

[Wezs78]   J. Wezska, "A survey of threshold selection techniques," *Comput. Graph. Image Processing*, **7** (1978).

[Wong78]   R. Y. Wong, E. L. Hall, "Scene matching with invariant moments," *Comput. Graph. Image Processing*, **8**, 1 (Aug. 1978).

[Wu83]   Z.Q. Wu, A. Rosenfeld, "Filtered projections as an aid in corner detection," *Pattern Recogn.*, **16**, 1 (1983).

[Yala85]   S. Yalamanchili, J. K. Aggarwal, "Analysis of a model for parallel image processing," *Pattern Recogn.*, **18**, 1 (1985), pp. 1-16.

[Yama78]   K. Yamamoto, S. Mori, "Recognition of handprinted characters by outermost point methods," *Proc. Fourth Int. Conf. on Pattern Recogn.*, Kyoto, Japan, 1978, pp. 794-796.

[Yee76]   Hsun Yee, G. Flachs, "Structural feature extraction by projections," *Region V IEEE Conf. Digest on Elec. Eng. for this Decade*, Austin, Texas, Apr. 1976, pp. 15-19.

Subject Index